The
BUCKEY BROTHERS

Building a Community Job by Job

GINA BUCKEY

Tony,
When I thought the book
was almost complete you
reminded me I needed
documentation. Thanks I
needed that guidance and
the other support you gave
me.
Gina Buckey

GB PUBLISHING
NEWARK, OHIO

DEDICATION

This book is dedicated to the Buckey Brothers.

Left to right: Robert Ernest Buckey, M. Gregg Buckey,
H. Carlos Buckey, and E. Ward Buckey.
Don Pound Photography.

First Edition

Copyright ©2019 • GB Publishing • Newark, Ohio

ISBN: 978-0-578-52409-2

CONTENTS

ABOUT THE AUTHOR

Gina Buckey, the daughter of R. E. Buckey, lives in Newark Ohio. She grew up in Newark and has lived most of her life there except for teaching elementary school in the Cincinnati area, instructing as a Clinical Instructor at The Ohio State College of Dentistry and working at Cuyahoga Community College in Cleveland as an Assistant Professor in the Dental Hygiene Department. She is a graduate of The Ohio State University with a Registered Dental Hygienist Certificate along with a Bachelor of Science Degree from the College of Education.

Gina was motivated to write this book after reading through R. E. Buckey's biography, diary, and his collection of photographs, newspaper articles and office papers.

Introduction

The book begins with a biography written by Robert E. Buckey in 1972. He describes his early life in Cambridge, Ohio and why he left The Ohio State University to begin estimating jobs and working at construction sites. He explains how a trip to Hebron, Ohio brought him to Newark where he was employed by Hawkins Construction Company.

In 1932, he started his own construction company. In 1943, he enlisted in the United States Army and in 1946, Buckey Brothers Construction Company was formed. Buckey Brothers specialized in commercial and industrial construction. For more than 25 years in business, they completed more than 2,000 jobs in Licking and surrounding counties.

Thanks go to R. E. Buckey for saving multiple files of photos, newspapers and newspaper clippings from his life and work. The office staff's papers were also of great help. Without the office records of the jobs completed, this book could not have been written.

Above
Charles Emory Buckey and
Alma Downey Buckey.

Left
Elijah Downey and
Julia Gregg Downey.

From the Buckey family collection.

CHAPTER I

R.E. BUCKEY'S BIOGRAPHY:
In His Own Words

Above
Ernest Buckey. Retiring from the construction business.
From the Buckey family collection.

I was born March 11, 1905 at the Old Cambridge Baptist Church area three miles south of Cambridge, Ohio. My sisters were Grace Ryder Buckey and Marian Buckey Peoples, an adopted sister and first cousin whose mother died during the 1918 flu epidemic. My brothers were H. Carlos Buckey, E. Ward Buckey, M. Gregg Buckey, A. Downey Buckey, twin of Gregg who died three days after birth.

My parents were Charles Emory Buckey, 1889-1960 and Alma Downey Buckey, 1891-1946. My maternal grandparents were Elijah Downey and Julia Gregg Downey. I had a faint memory of Grandmother Downey who died in 1909. Grandfather Downey lived in Hebron, Ohio and married Janie House in later life. He suffered a stroke and was confined to bed for the last seven years of his life. He died in the late 20's or early 30's. My paternal grandparents were William Buckey and Elizabeth Gander Buckey. I remembered Grandfather Buckey quite well. He died approximately 1912 or 1913. Grandmother Buckey lived with her unmarried daughter, Jane, for several years after his death.

Weimer Gregg was my maternal great grandmother who I remembered as an elderly lady usually dressed in black, but I have no knowledge concerning Great Grandfather Gregg. Johnathon Gander and Susan Hickle Gander, my paternal grandparents, I remember because we sat on their front porch on Clark Street in Cambridge, Ohio and watched a circus parade go by. They died one day apart at approximate age of 90 and I well remember going to the double funeral.

My early life was very happy living on a 32-acre farm. Mother was very affectionate and dad a very hard-working man. He was a coal miner, worked 10 hours a day, six days a week, and in mid-winter he did not see sunlight except on Sunday. He always had a large garden and kept chickens, cows and one horse. Chickens always appealed to me and Dad always tried to have a nest of eggs hatch on my March 11 birthday.

At age six, I started to school at nearby Beech Grove School. It was a one-room, wood building, and the pupils were divided into six classes, using the six McGuffey readers.

Older pupils would be sixteen years old and I remember two of the older boys who chewed tobacco and spit in a can on the floor between their double seats. Heat was provided by a pot-bellied stove and girls and boys were seated on opposite sides of the room. Many of the students were foreign (Slavish, Hungarian, etc.) and some started to school with no knowledge of the English language. After two years in the one-room building, a new brick, two-room school was built across the road on land donated by my father and mother. I completed my elementary schooling there.

Above
Ernest Buckey with his mother, Alma Buckey.
From the Buckey family collection.

Below
The fifth, sixth, seventh and eighth grade students of Beech Grove School, Cambridge, Ohio. Ernest Buckey is standing in the back row, fourth from the left.
From the Buckey family collection.

Entered Cambridge High School in Sept. 1918. Walked approximately 1 ½ miles to the Cambridge-Byesville Street car line (stop 8) and rode the trolley to Cambridge for the first two years. Roads were unpaved and walking was quite difficult in muddy weather. I remember joining with other students in a spontaneous parade at the signing of the Armistice (Nov. 11, 1918). Graduated from Cambridge High School, June 1922. Worked as a laborer during the summer shoveling gravel into a mixer to pave the road past our house.

Enrolled in Ohio State University, Oct. 1, 1922, in the College of Agriculture. Washed dishes at a boarding club to help pay my way through school.

Above
Ernest Buckey's high school graduation photo, 1922.
From the Buckey family collection.

Left
Autumn Quarter Expenses, 1922.
From the Buckey family collection.

Below
R. E. Buckey at The Ohio State University Stadium.
From the Buckey family collection.

Our family replaced the old unpainted house (with two pine trees in front) with a new seven-room house in 1922. At that time, electric service was not available, but the house was wired and arrangements were made for future inside plumbing. It was 1928 before these services were installed.

Above
Tearing down the old Buckey family home in 1922.
From the Buckey family collection.

Left
The new Buckey family home.
From the Buckey family collection.

During the summer of 1923, I got a job as a laborer on construction of Byesville High School that made a profound change in my life plans. I became very much interested in construction and changed my course at Ohio State from Agricultural to Architectural Engineering. Worked at construction during the summer of 1924 at New Matamoris, Ohio, and began learning the bricklaying trade as an apprentice. In March of 1925, Mr. H. H. Criswell, a contractor, talked me into leaving school and coming into his office to help with estimating, as well as working on construction jobs. My salary was $25.00 per week. The first job I was assigned to was the construction of a bakery building at the Boy's Industrial School, Lancaster Ohio."

From 1925 to 1928, I worked on various construction jobs in Barnesville, Quaker City, St. Clairsville, Steubenville, Tiffen [sic], and Carrolton. During the summer of 1928, I brought mother over to visit her father in Hebron and while there I drove over to Newark (my first time there) and found Hawkins Construction Company building the South First Street office for the Ohio Power Co. They offered me a job ($75 per week – very good for those times) and I moved to Newark, boarding and rooming at 280 Hudson Avenue.

JANUARY, 1928

Tuesday 10

Took Mom to Grandpa's. Went to Newark & was offered a Job by Hawkins

Above
From Ernest's diary January 1928.
From the Buckey family collection.

Below
Ernest Buckey, twenty two years old, with his automobile.
From the Buckey family collection.

PROGRESS PHOTO NO. I
AUGUST 28TH 1930

LIBRARY — OHIO UNIV — 4-17
JAMES WILLIAM THOMAS — ARCH
THE HAWKINS CONST. CO — CON

Above & Left
Progress photographs of the construction of the Chubb Memorial Library August 28, 1930 to April 17, 1931. Howell and Thomas architects and built by the Hawkins Construction Company. Various photographers. (These photos survived the 1959 Newark flood.)

From the Buckey family collection.

Sigma Chi Fraternity House
Denison University.

Sigma Chi Memory Room

Sigma Chi Chapter Room

#305 - SIGMA CHI FRATERNITY
DENISON UNIV. - GRANVILLE, OHIO

GRANGER & BOLLENBACHER
ARCHITECTS CHICAGO, ILL

THE HAWKINS CONSTRUCTION COMPANY
CONTRACTORS NEWARK, OHIO

I worked part time in the office and in the summer of 1929, I was placed in charge as construction superintendent of the new Roosevelt Junior High School on Mt. Vernon Road. After completion of this school, I was superintendent of construction on Chubb Memorial Library, Ohio University, Athens Ohio.

I supervised construction of the Sigma Chi Fraternity, Phi Gamma Fraternity and the new entrance and roadways, all at Denison University.

Above
Hawkins Construction Company.
All photos this page from the Buckey family collection.

Above & Left
Phi Gamma Delta Fraternity
Denison University.

Photos from the Buckey family collection.

Above & Left
Entrance to Denison University.
Photos from the Buckey family collection.

In 1932, I was masonry foreman on the Licking County Tuberculosis Hospital. Depression hit in 1929, but I was not greatly affected by it due to previous negotiated contracts until in 1933 and all of 1934.

On June 14, 1934, I married Virginia Woltjen. In the summer of 1935, I decided to start as a building contractor and the first sizable contract was construction of the Hebron Gymnasium. I continued in the contracting field as an individual until the spring of 1943. In August 1937, a daughter Gina Ann Buckey was born and in August of 1940, Roberta Ernestine came into the family.

In May 1943, I enlisted in the army with a direct commission of Captain and reported to Fort Belvoir on June 4. After officer training, I was made company Commander of colored troops in Corps of Engineers. I trained troops in Monroe, N. C., Fort Fisher, N. C., and Camp Forest, Tenn. In October 1944, we left San Francisco by boat for the Pacific Theater and spent nine months on Biak Island, New Guinea. Our Battalion followed the First Cavalry Division through Leyte and into Manila. Most of our assignments were maintaining and extending air strips.

I left Manila for home November 29, 1945 and arrived in San Francisco, January 1, 1946. Mother's death came only about two months after I got home."

Above
Captain R. E. Buckey.
From the Buckey family collection.

Left
Page from the government book: *I've been Around.*
From the Buckey family collection.

On my way!

Name ROBERT E. BUCKEY

Address 112 LINDEN AVE

NEWARK, OHIO

Date of Registration for Selective Service_____

Date of Classification by Local Board_____

Order Number_____ Classified in Class_____

I was in!

Date JUNE 4, 1943   Serial Number O-924904

Arrived at FORT BELVOIR VA

Locations of Assignment Before Embarkation_____

JUNE 4 - AUG. 7 1943   Ft Belvoir VA

AUG. 8 - AUG 29 1943   Camp Claiborne LA.

AUG 29 - Dec 14 1943   Camp Sutton NC

Dec 15 1943 - Jan 29 1944   Smokey Mountains, Tenn

Jan 30 - Feb 27 1944   Tennessee Maneuver Area

Feb 28 - May 5 1944   Camp Sutton NC

May 5 - Aug 25 1944   Fort Fisher NC

Aug 25 - Oct 12 1944   Camp Sutton N.C.

Oct 12 - Oct 27 1944   Enroute to #AY Camp Stoneman Calif

In March 1946, we formed Buckey Brothers, Inc. consisting of myself and brothers Carlos, Ward and Gregg to engage in building work.

We conducted this business for more than 25 years with absolutely no friction between us at any time. Jobs completed include the Park National Bank, Newark Y. W. C. A., Benjamin Franklin School, Lakewood High School, Dow Chemical Co., Standard Register and more than 2000 smaller projects. In December of 1971, we dissolved our corporation and discontinued business.

Virginia and I started housekeeping in a small apartment at 44 East Church Street (opposite Second Presbyterian Church). Lived there almost three years at a rental of twenty dollars per month with heat furnished. In spring of 1937, we moved to 112 Linden Avenue in a six-room rented house and lived there for 26 years. In 1963 we rented an apartment in the Hudson House, 220 Hudson Avenue where we are living at this date. In March of 1950, we purchased a lake-front house at Harbor Hills and continue to spend our summers there.

Three dogs have brought a lot of happiness to our lives: Wally, 1937-1938, a Scottie who was killed by a car, Blackie, 1944-1957, a black terrier who died of old age and Misti, 1960, a silver French poodle who is still with us.

Civic affiliations I belong to are listed below:

Acme Lodge F & AM - Blue Lodge - Chapter & Council

Elks Lodge - Joined in 1946

Newark Chamber of Commerce - Director, 1950-1955

Newark Rotary Club - President, 1954-1955

American Legion Post 85 - Joined in 1946

First Federal Savings & Loan - Director

Second Presbyterian Church - Members

Presently, my occupation is retired.

To my (deceased) Parents, Wife and Family, Relatives and Friends - Thanks for helping make my life so interesting and happy.

R. Ernest Buckey

R. Ernest Buckey's biography, dated July 21, 1972, was transcribed from his original writing, with slight editing at the beginning.

From the Buckey family collection.

R. E. Buckey's work truck.
From the Buckey family collection.

CHAPTER 2

1935 - 1942

R. E. BUCKEY, CONTRACTOR

BUCKEY GETS SCHOOL JOB

The contract for the construction of a $50,000 three-story addition to the Amanda school building in Fairfield county has been awarded R. E. Buckey, Newark contractor. Richards, McCarty & Bulford, Columbus, are the architects. The building will be of fireproof construction throughout.

Work will be started within the next few days, and will be rushed to completion as quickly as the weather permits.

Firm Gets Contract.

The general contract for the fireproof addition to the Ashley village school building in Delaware county has been awarded

to R. E. Buckey, Newark contractor. The building will involve an expenditure of $72,000 and includes the erection of a combination gymnasium and auditorium and eight classrooms. Work has been started on the project and will be completed by Nov 1

Right
Ashley School 1937. (This photo survived the 1959 Newark flood.) *Photos from the Buckey family collection.*

Robert Ernest Buckey, Ernie as he was known, began his construction business in Newark, Ohio working from his home, first at 44 W. Church Street and later at 112 Linden Avenue. His work extended into Coshocton County with the contract for the construction of the new Union Rural School building, located at Preston's Corners. The winning bid was $72,949. For the bid of $50,000 the Amanda Board of Education in Fairfield County awarded him the contract for their school addition only after the winning bidder for the job withdrew his bid. In Delaware County, he built the addition to the Ashley Village School which included a gymnasium, auditorium and eight classrooms for the cost of $72,000.

Further north on Lake Erie, he constructed the bridge abutments for the Erie Avenue Bridge in Lorain, Ohio.

Left & Below
Erie Avenue Bridge in Lorain, 1940. (These photos survived the 1959 Newark flood.)

Photos from the Buckey family collection.

Works completed in Licking County during this time were the Hebron School addition, remodeling of the Makris Brothers Restaurant, remodeling Gutliph and Henderson Funeral Home and remodeling the Serocco Avenue substation for the Ohio Power Company. His first sizable contract was a 60-foot, three-story, brick-and-steel addition to the main building of the Pharis Tire and Rubber Plant.

In 1937, the F. W. Woolworth Company's store addition was completed, and for the Newark Advocate Printing Company, he added the third floor addition, 50 feet by 100 feet, to provide additional space for their commercial printing department. The Newark Bus Terminal was completed on schedule under the supervision of R. E. Buckey Contractor. In 1938, Buckey's bid was low for renovating the Newark Post Office. For a bid of $8,658, the job consisted of painting the interior and exterior, enlarging the vestibule and miscellaneous repairs. Bids from five contractors ranged up to $15,000. The government allocated less than $8,000 for this work so a special representative of the Treasury had to decide whether additional funds were available for the work or all bids were to be rejected and again advertised. Since the contract was awarded without rebidding, the additional monies were made available.

Below & Right
Clippings from the Newark Advocate.

From the Buckey family collection.

In 1942, an Owens Corning warehouse was built by R. E. Buckey Contractor.

Left, Below & Right
Progress photographs of the construction of the Owens Corning Warehouse on April 10, May 25 and August 3, 1942. (These photos survived the 1959 Newark flood.)

Photos from the Buckey family collection.

Owens Corning Warehouse
Photo no 6 Aug 3 1942
R.E. Buckey Contractor

Right
Clippings from the
Newark Advocate.

*From the Buckey
family collection.*

CONGRATULATIONS

OWENS-CORNING

FIBERGLAS

CORPORATION

*Total Production
means Total Victory*

• We are proud of the part we have
played in construction and building
maintenance at the Owens-Corning
plant IN THE PAST.

• . . . Proud, also, of our PRESENT
connection in the same capacity . . .

• . . . and look forward to being further able to serve this vital war indus-
try in THE FUTURE.

R. E. Buckey

CONTRACTOR

It Pays To Employ a Responsible Contractor

INDUSTRIAL and
COMMERCIAL
CONSTRUCTION
A SPECIALTY!

112 Linden Ave.

Phone 24364

AN ACKNOWLEDGMENT

⎡ We take pride in having been chosen
⎢ as General Contractors in the con-
⎢ struction of the modern Newark Con-
⎣ sumers Gas Company office building. ⎤

ITS COMPLETION ADDS ANOTHER ACHIEVEMENT
TO OUR LIST WHICH INCLUDES—

UNION RURAL SCHOOL BUILDING, COSHOCTON COUNTY
EDEN TOWNSHIP SCHOOL, LICKING COUNTY
ASHLEY SCHOOL ADDITION, ASHLEY, OHIO
HEBRON SCHOOL ADDITION, HEBRON, OHIO
ERIE AVE. BRIDGE ABUTMENTS, LORAIN, OHIO
ADDITION TO THE PHARIS TIRE & RUBBER CO. PLANT
MAKRIS BROS. RESTAURANT
REMODELING OF GUTLIPH & HENDERSON FUNERAL HOME
SEROCCO AVE. SUBSTATION FOR THE OHIO POWER CO.
F. W. WOOLWORTH CO. STORE ADDITION
THIRD FLOOR ADDITION FOR THE ADVOCATE PRINTING CO.

When you consider construction work,
we suggest that you consult us for
accurate estimates of cost.

R. E. BUCKEY

★ COMMERCIAL AND INDUSTRIAL CONSTRUCTION

112 LINDEN AVENUE · -:- · PHONE 24364

23

Chapter 3

1943 - 1945

Captain R.E. Buckey and the Army Corps of Engineers

Above
Bombs on Biak Island before the storage area was built.

Left Top
Clearing the jungle.

Left Bottom
General area.

Right
Bomb Storage after the jungle was cleared.

Photos from the Buckey family collection.

Ernest enlisted in the Army without informing his family of his intentions. Captain Buckey trained "colored" troops in North Carolina and Tennessee. He left from San Francisco on October 27, 1944 and arrived at Biak Island, Dutch West Indies on November 20, 1944. Biak Island is located about 900 miles southeast of Japan and the Allies used this Southwest Pacific route to advance to the Philippines. His photos show their typical job of clearing the jungle to erect temporary shelters for bomb storage.

He was also in Manila, the capital of the Philippines, which is on Luzon Island, and sent home photos of the bombing destruction there.

Left
The burned-out Manila Hotel.
From the Buckey family collection.

Left
Custom building where Japanese placed charges.
From the Buckey family collection.

To be with him during his training, the Buckey family traveled south, first to a rental in Monroe, North Carolina. Then while stationed at Fort Fisher, North Carolina, they settled and rented a beach house at Carolina Beach with other military families.

During the fall of 1944, the family returned to Linden Avenue. School became his daughters' life and they looked forward to walking home for lunch, anticipating mail from their father. Mail was delivered twice a day and the girls again looked forward to the afternoon delivery. Letters from Captain Buckey to his daughters contained drawings. They were able to enjoy the letters their mother read to them, filling in her pauses, as they identified the pictures their father had drawn.

Above
Captain Buckey with a Japanese gun.
From the Buckey family collection.

CHAPTER 4

1946 - 1971

BUCKEY BROTHERS

CONTRACTORS

ANNOUNCING....

the formation of Buckey Brothers Company, which will again operate a general contracting business in the city of Newark.

Specializing in commercial and industrial construction under the name of

CONTRACTORS

NEWARK, OHIO.   PHONE 24364

"It Pays To Employ A Responsible Contractor"

| R. E. BUCKEY | H. CARLOS BUCKEY | GREGG BUCKEY |

Above
A clipping from the City Note Page of the Newark Advocate.
From the Buckey family collection.

Left Top
Buckey Brothers office.

Left Bottom
Cement plant and storage shed.
Photos from the Buckey family collection.

Upon his return to the states, Ernest had attorney George McDonald prepare the papers of incorporation for the Buckey Brothers in March of 1946. The business consisted of R. E. Buckey and his three brothers. Carl came to Newark in 1928, working for another contractor on the Midland Theatre building. Gregg came to Newark in 1935 and Ward joined his brothers after the company was formed.

The new business began with a capital of $50,000. Buckey Brothers was incorporated for $100,000 and authorized to issue one thousand shares of stock with no par value. Temporary offices were located at 112 Linden Avenue. Officers of the newly formed Buckey Brothers were: President R. E. Buckey, Vice President H. Carlos Buckey, Secretary E. Ward Buckey, and Treasurer M. Gregg Buckey. Key personnel were the Job Superintendents E. Stanton Hilleary, H. Clair Orr, and Fred Martin; the Yard Superintendent Pete Paublos; the Office Manager David A. Allen, and Bookkeeper Willard Paul Huffman.

The new location for the Buckey Brothers became 171 Riverside Drive, Newark, Ohio. Buildings used for their construction projects included a small office building, a cement plant with a storage shed, the Yard (a warehouse) and a lumber shed.

Left
The Yard.

Left
The lumber shed.

Photos from the Buckey family collection.

1947-1950

FROM WCLT TO ST. FRANCIS DE SALES GYMNASIUM

Building the WCLT radio station, which went on the air August, 1947, was the first job for the brothers. On March 20, 1948 a tornado hit Licking County around 3:00 pm and brought down the 330-foot tower. The discussion at the dinner table that evening was whether the concrete had failed. The finding was that the concrete held and the tower metal twisted during the tornado. A new tower went up in1949 and an addition to the station was added in 1966.

Left
Job 1 New WCLT Radio Station. (This photo survived the 1959 Newark flood.)
Photo from the Buckey family collection.

Below
Job 1 WCLT Radio Station, the tower down.
Clippiung from the Newark Advocate.

The Newark Baseball Company hired the Buckeys to construct Arnold Park which was located on the site of the present YMCA. It was the home of the Newark Yankees who played in the Ohio Indiana League from 1948 to 1951. They were a farm team for The New York Yankees. On July 17, 1951, the Newark team withdrew from the league.

Above & Left
Job 79 The Newark Baseball Company. (These photos survived the 1959 Newark flood.)

Photos from the Buckey family collection.

Right
Job 79 The Newark Baseball Company.

Clippings from the City Note Page of the Newark Advocate.

WRESTLING
Arnold Park
8:30 p. m.
Thurs., Aug. 18

TOMMY FOX
vs.
WHITEY WALBERG

GIRLS

MAE WESTON
vs.
ANN LA VERNE

GORGEOUS GUS
vs.
GEORGE O'HARA

RINGSIDE CHAIRS $1.25
GENERAL ADMISSION .$1.00
CHILDREN ....$ .50

Gorgeous Gus, the wrestling
bear. A 300 pound black bear
undefeated by any man.

NEGRO BASEBALL GAME
MONDAY, JUNE 27TH
ARNOLD PARK   GAME TIME 8:30 P. M.

BROOKLYN CUBAN GIANTS
vs.
NEW ORLEANS CREOLES

(Featuring TONY STONE, stellar female athlete who will
start the game at second base for the New Orleans Creoles.)

Box Seats $1.00 — General Admission 50c

WRESTLING at ARNOLD PARK

SATURDAY, JUNE 4th — 8:00 p. m.

2 — FEATURE ATTRACTIONS — 2

TAG TEAM EVENT

IRISH MIKE McGEE..........of Cedar Rapids, Iowa
BILLY FOX...................of Cleveland, Ohio
GEORGE O'HARA ....of Amarillo, Texas
JACK VANSKY ....of Buffalo, New York

MAIN EVENT

IVAN RASPUTIN OF RUSSIA
— vs. —
DR. E. MESKE OF AKRON, OHIO

Two Prices Only ....Gen. Adm., $1.00; Ringside, $1.25

See the new arena at the ball park — every seat close — no
screen between you and the action.

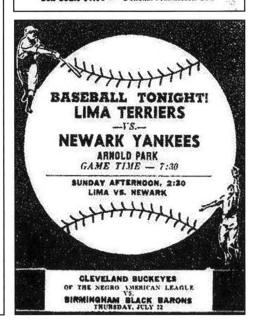

BASEBALL TONIGHT!
LIMA TERRIERS
—vs.—
NEWARK YANKEES
ARNOLD PARK
GAME TIME — 7:30

SUNDAY AFTERNOON, 2:30
LIMA VS. NEWARK

CLEVELAND BUCKEYES
OF THE NEGRO AMERICAN LEAGUE
VS.
BIRMINGHAM BLACK BARONS
THURSDAY, JULY 22

Homes were needed for returning military servicemen and Production-Built Homes hired Buckey Brothers in 1947 to pour foundations and do chimney work for 50 homes on South 34th Street.

Powell Electric, at 31 North Fifth Street, was remodeled by the brothers for the owner, Tom Powell.

Above
Job 169 Powell Electric Company.
A clipping from the City Note Page of the Newark Advocate. From the Buckey family collection.

Left
Job 169 Powell Electric Company.
A clipping from the Newark Advocate. From the Buckey family collection.

Above & Left
Job 169 Powell Electric Company. (These photos survived the 1959 Newark flood.)
From the Buckey family collection.

The new Dog Pound was built on Dog Leg Road RFD #5, Newark.

Above & Left
Job 187 The Dog Pound.
(These photos survived the
1959 Newark flood.)
From the Buckey family collection.

Buckey Brothers' bid of $128,576 for the ten classrooms at the new Utica Grade School was the lowest of five submitted. When the Utica Herald newspaper editor visited in the fall of 1948, he saw 21 men, skilled workmen, bricklayers, carpenters, plumbers, etc. busy at various tasks. Construction was slowed because of poor weather conditions and a delay in the delivery of the steel roof joists. The final cost for the school, completed in August 1949, was $129,885. The newspaper clipping shows the old grade school in the background.

BUCKEY BROTHERS
General Contractors

Congratulate The Residents of the
Utica-Washington School District on Their
Fine New Elementary Building

We Are Proud To Have Had So Large a Share In Building This Splendid New Structure for the Boys and Girls of the Utica-Washington School District

Commercial And Industrial Construction a Specialty

Buckey Brothers

General Contractors, Phone 3533   Builder's Supplies, Phone 3362
171 RIVERSIDE DRIVE, NEWARK, OHIO

"It Pays To Employ a Reliable Contractor"

Left
Job 240 Utica Elementary School.

A clipping from the Newark Advocate. From the Buckey family collection.

During December 1948, Permanente Metals had machine foundations and other work done on what later became Kaiser Aluminum. For this job, Buckey Brothers had eighty-five men doing the construction work that included pouring 1,500 yards of concrete. The work involved setting piles and laying concrete for a three-story high breakdown mill for reducing large aluminum ingots to small rods and bars. The work was completed in less than 80 days. Permanente Metals, a Kaiser Aluminum Subsidiary, was acquired through a lease from the War Assets Administration and the Newark plant included 36 buildings with 300 acres of land. The plant was built in 1942 and operated during the war by the Aluminum Company of America. The Buckeys then poured more machinery foundations there in 1950.

Left
Job 281 Permanente Metals. Machinery Foundations.
From the Buckey family collection.

Permanente Metals Plant, Newark, Ohio

Left
Job 281 Permanente Metals.
A postcard. From the Buckey family collection.

In March of 1949, an entire two-bedroom Lustron house, 31 feet by 35 feet, was loaded on a truck, ready to be set up at 381 North 21st Street by the Buckey Brothers, who had been contracted to build Lustron Homes. Attending a four-day school in Columbus were H. Clair Orr, Fred D. Martin, and H. Carlos Buckey to learn how to erect the five-room house. The house had 1,000 square feet of living space, weighed ten tons and was placed on a slab.

These were all steel enamel constructed, prefabricated homes manufactured in the former Curtis-Wright buildings in Columbus. A new Lustron house cost $6,000 to $10,000 without the cost of a building lot. They had many built-in features, such as a built-in, under-the-sink Thor Washing Machine that, with the installation of a special rack, did double-duty as a dishwasher, a luxury at the time. Lustron declared bankruptcy in 1950. For a period of time after its completion, the 21st Street Lustron House was opened by the Twentieth Century Club for public viewing, daily from 2:00 pm to 10:00 pm. There was an admission fee of 25 cents and those monies went to the club's charities.

A second Lustron house went up at 168 North 30th Street shortly after the 21st Street home was completed.

Above
Job 282 The Lustron house arrived.

A clipping from the Newark Advocate. From the Buckey family collection.

Left
Job 282 Right half of the front side of the 21st Street Lustron House.

A photo from Robert and Patricia McGaughy.

Cozy Cottages Travel by Truck These Days

Left
Job 282 The Lustron House.

A clipping from the City Note Page of the Newark Advocate. From the Buckey family collection.

St. Francis de Sales new gymnasium and auditorium was built at the rear of Slattery Hall, facing Pearl Street. There was seating capacity for 800 and the basketball floor was 80 feet by 44 feet. The basketball court was planned for two practice courts for use by smaller children. In a found newspaper clipping, The Reverend Father Edward A. McGinty, St. Francis' pastor stated, The cornerstone was to be laid July, 1949 by the Most Reverend Michael J. Ready, D. D., Bishop of the Columbus Diocese.

Cornerstone of Parish Hall To Be Laid Tuesday

The cornerstone for St. Francis de Sale's new gymnasium-auditorium will be laid at 11 a. m. Tuesday by the Most Rev. Michael J. Ready, D.D., bishop of the Columbus Diocese, it was announced by the Rev. Fr. Edward A. McGinty, St. Francis pastor.

Master of ceremonies will be the Very Rev. Msgr. Roland T. Winel, secretary to Bishop Ready.

The new building is being erected on parish property at the rear of Slattery Hall, facing Pearl Street. With a seating capacity of 800, the gym's basketball floor will be 80 by 44 feet of hard maple. It can be converted into two practice courts for smaller children.

There will also be two standard sized classrooms, social meeting rooms, and a kitchen. Locker rooms will be placed under the stage, which will have a depth of 31 feet.

John P. Schooley of the firm of Sims, Cornelius, and Schooley of Columbus is the architect for the new structure. General contractors are Buckey Brothers of Newark with O. D. Hollar and Son, plumbing, and John Thornton, electric.

Above
Job 340 St. Francis de Sales gymnasium.

A 1949 clipping from the Newark Advocate. From the Buckey family collection.

Left Top
Job 340 St. Francis de Sales gymnasium.

From the Buckey family collection.

Left Bottom
Job 340 St. Francis de Sales gymnasium 2003.

From the Buckey family collection.

1951-1955

FROM NEWARK A&P TO FIRESTONE STORE

Construction began on the Newark A & P Super Market on South Fifth Street. The Newark store was owned by the four brothers. Their grand opening was October 20, 1950.

While working on the additions to three schools and building a farm shop for the Coshocton Board of Education, the opportunity became available for the Buckeys to purchase land at the corner of Third and Walnut Streets to build an A & P Super Market for Buckey Realty. The building, 75 feet by 100 feet, was of standard type construction, rectangular with the front facing on Third Street. There was no basement, but provision was made for equipment and storage with the construction of a special room at the rear of the main salesroom. A parking lot large enough to accommodate 50 automobiles was paved adjacent to the building.

Top
Job 420 A&P Super Market. Grand Opening. (This clipping survived the 1959 Newark flood).

A clipping from the Newark Advocate. From the Buckey family collection.

Above
Job 420 A&P Super Market. Grand Opening.

A clipping from the Newark Advocate. From the Buckey family collection.

In the early 1950s, the Buckeys remodeled the Newark Township School and built an addition to what later was known as North Elementary School. A new gymnasium and auditorium were added to the Fulton School, along with a four-classroom addition. At this time, these were Newark Township Schools. Newark Township School became North Elementary, in the Newark City School District, and Fulton School became part of the Heath City School District. In 1956, the Fulton School Bus Garage was built.

Buckey Brothers advertised they were specialists in commercial and industrial construction and many times Ernie stated they did not do any residential work. However, in 1951 they were persuaded by Games Slayter to build an addition onto Old Locust Farm, at the cost of $43,004.

The Buckeys had their photos taken for the 1952, Newark Sesquicentennial Souvenir Book. Their advertisement in the Souvenir Book said, *Long after our name is forgotten... the products of our labor will continue to serve the needs of future generations. For 17 years, Buckey Brothers have employed competent craftsmen, assuring the buyer that he is receiving the most for his money.*

R. E. BUCKEY   CARLOS BUCKEY   GREGG BUCKEY   WARD BUCKEY

Above
The Buckey Brothers.
From the Buckey family collection.

Venturing south in 1952 to Washington Court House, they built a building for Med-O-Pure Dairy and two years later an addition was added. Another addition followed in 1960. There, Med-O-Pure processed and distributed milk products. Some of their milks were Standard, Homogenized, Golden Guernsey and Gurn-Z-Gold. Their ice cream was advertised as Med-O-Pure Ice Cream and Bing Crosby Ice Cream. Later the Dairy was owned by Avoset.

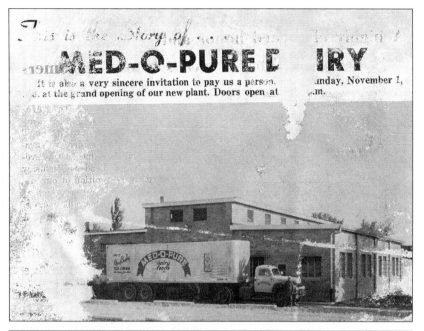

Above
Job 777 Med-O-Pure Dairy Open House with advertising on a milk carton. (This item survived the 1959 Newark flood).
From the Buckey family collection.

Left
Job 777 Med-O-Pure Dairy. Advertising clipping. (This item survived the 1959 Newark flood).
From the Buckey family collection.

Left
Job 1003 Med-O-Pure Dairy became Avoset Dairy.
From the Buckey family collection.

Below
Job 777 Med-O-Pure Dairy Location. (This item survived the 1959 Newark flood).
From the Buckey family collection.

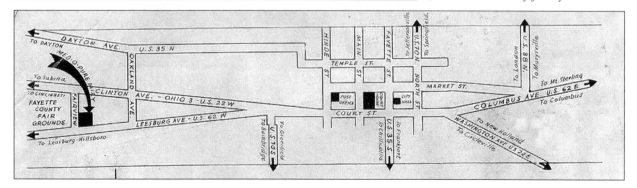

On March 2, 1953 in Granville, the College Town House built in the 1880's suffered a fire loss of $20,000 which was fully covered by insurance. Buckey Brothers worked to restore the building as it was before the fire and completed the work by June 1.

Walter Deutsch hired the Buckeys to construct a new building designed specifically for his business, Postal Printing. Located in the rear of the business was the modern printing and lithography department. The first floor had their stationery store and the office. In the lower level there was a complete line of office furniture along with a storage area. Their grand opening was in 1953.

Below
Job 832 Postal Printing Company's Grand Opening.
A clipping from the Newark Advocate. From the Buckey family collection.

Ambition of 20 Years Realized

New Home of Postal Printing Company, Owned by Walter Deutsch, Now Ready

Dedication of the new addition to Jacksontown School was held on Sunday April 25, 1954. A $140,000 bond issue was passed by the community providing for four new classrooms and office space. Around 100 children in first, second and sixth grade moved into the new addition. Among those participating in the dedication were H. Carlos Buckey who presented the token keys to Joseph Baker, architect, who then passed them to Delbert Hoskinson, the president of the Jacksontown Board of Education.

Below
Job 855 Jacksontown School addition.
A clipping from the Newark Advocate. From the Buckey family collection.

Participating in the dedication ceremonies were, (seated, from left to right), Willard Shrider, president of the Jacksontown Community Club; D. L Hoskinson, president of the board of education; Ralph Billett, executive head; (standing), Harold Sebold, superintendent of Licking County Schools (former executive head at Jacksontown); Floyd Gale, pastor of the Jacksontown M. E. Church; Joseph Baker, architect; H. Carlos Buckey, vice president of the Buckey Brothers Construction Company; and Dr. F. H McKelvey, the featured speaker and the director of the summer session at Ohio University.

The city saw the new Benjamin Franklin Junior High School being built in the south end of Newark. A photograph from October 28, 1954 shows the tower being constructed at the rear of the building. The building was completed in just over a year and a half. Sidewalks and curbs were poured in 1955.

Benjamin Franklin Junior High School

Left
Job 940 Completed tower.

A clipping from the Newark Advocate. From the Buckey family collection.

Above & Left
Job 940 Benjamin Franklin Junior High School tower being built. (These photos survived the 1959 Newark flood.)

Photos from the Buckey family collection.

St. Edwards, the first Catholic Church built in Granville, was completed in 11 months on six acres east of the village. The church was 40 feet by 80 feet and had the seating capacity for 210, with additional seating in the choir. Pews and other special woodwork were done by L. A. Schwarzkopf of Granville. On October 30, 1954, a procession proceeded from the old chapel on the corner of Pearl and Broadway to the new church east of the village where Bishop Ready laid the cornerstone. On March 20, 1955, the church was dedicated by Bishop Ready to an overflow crowd. At that time, St. Edwards served 65 local families and Denison students. Completed by the Buckeys in 1956 were the Rectory and Common Rooms.

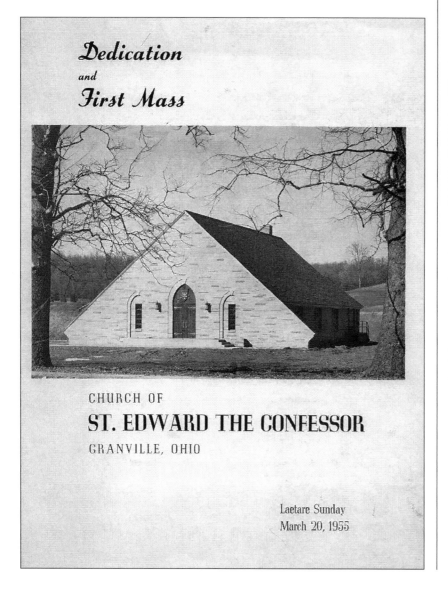

Dedication
and
First Mass

CHURCH OF
ST. EDWARD THE CONFESSOR
GRANVILLE, OHIO

Laetare Sunday
March 20, 1955

Above
Job 960 St. Edwards Church under Construction.
From the Buckey family collection.

Left
Job 960 St. Edwards Church. Cover of the Dedication Program.
From the Buckey family collection.

A ribbon was cut by Mayor Swank for the grand opening of the expanded Firestone store at the corner of Hudson Avenue and Locust Street. Orchids were given to the women and a three-day sale followed the September 30, 1955 ceremonies.

Grand Opening at Firestone Store

Left
Job 1040 Firestone Store. Attending the Grand Opening Ceremony, left to right: Sam Goddard, Commercial Sales; R. E. Buckey, general contractor; Ron Hefner, manager of the Newark store; V. P. Murray, district supervisor; Mayor Swank; and M. L. Gerould, district manager.

A clipping from the Newark Advocate. From the Buckey family collection.

1956-1960

From St. John's Evangelical Church to National Gas and Oil Company

St. John's Evangelical Church was dedicated March 10, 1957. This dedication was for the second unit of the church. The first unit, not a Buckey build, was dedicated August 3, 1952. All the finances used for these two buildings were given on a volunteer

Below
Job 1155 St. John's Evangelical Church.
From the Buckey family collection.

basis without help from fundraising events or programs. The tower in the front contained the three bells moved from the old church on the corner of Fifth and Poplar. Gothic architecture was the design of the exterior and interior.

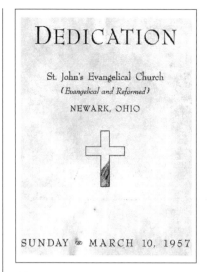

DEDICATION

St. John's Evangelical Church
(Evangelical and Reformed)
NEWARK, OHIO

SUNDAY ∞ MARCH 10, 1957

Above
Job 1155 St. John's Evangelical Church. Cover of the Dedication Program.
From the Buckey family collection.

Left & Below
Job 1155 St. John's Evangelical Church.
From the Buckey family collection.

On Augustine T. Wehrle's 500-acre farm, six miles south of Newark in Union Township, a training school for future priests and brothers was built. Saints Peter and Paul Seminary was where high school, college and theology classes were held. Buckey Brothers built the school and other facilities to house 100 students and the faculty. Time was donated each Saturday for eight weeks painting the interior and laying tile floors by the Newark Council #721 of the Church of the Blessed Sacrament, Knights of Columbus and the Holy Name Society. This was the first of the Saints Peter and Paul Missionaries to be built in America. Bishop Michael J. Ready laid the cornerstone on July 23, 1956 and the school began in the fall of 1959.

Right Top
Job 1177 Saints Peter and Paul Seminary.
A clipping from the Newark Advocate. From the Buckey family collection.

Right Bottom
Job 1177 Saints Peter and Paul Seminary. A Postcard.
From the Buckey family collection.

Above
Job 1177 Saints Peter and Paul Seminary.
An aerial photo from Ronald Sherwood.

Church Dignitaries Will Dedicate College

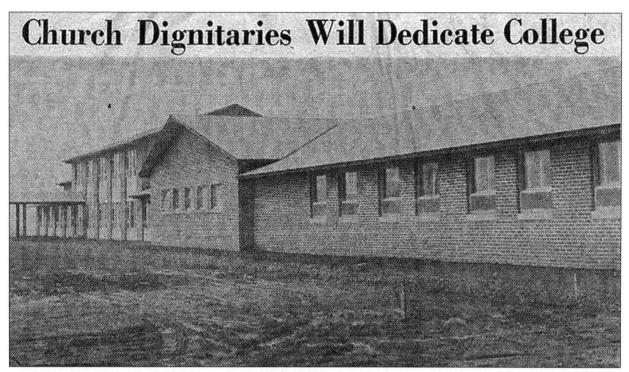

For $15,000, Herbert Murphy sold land to R. E. Buckey who built a Texaco Service Station, the first in the Newark area, where Granville Road and West Church Street met. This location was known as Dugway. John Gressle and Texaco jointly held the grand opening on November 17, 1956. The land and building were leased by the Texas Oil Company for 15 years.

Above
Job 1180 Texaco Service Station.

A clipping from the City Note Page of the Newark Advocate. From the Buckey family collection.

Left
Job 1180 Texaco Service Station.

Congratulatory advertisement from the Newark Advocate. From the Buckey family collection.

Everett D. Reese awarded the contract to build the new Park National Bank to the Buckey Brothers. In early 1957, the groundbreaking was held and Mr. Reese said, We are pleased to award the bids to local contractors, and we are also happy that the new bank will incorporate so many of our local products. At that time, the total cost of the construction was not disclosed. On May 17, 1957 220 yards of concrete were poured for the foundation. The pour began at five o'clock in the morning and concluded at six o'clock in the evening, using Buckey Brothers' three trucks. The cornerstone was laid September 7, 1957. In 1968, the second floor was remodeled for the Trust Department.

Groundbreaking for Park National's "new" office – Early 1957

Above
Job 1230 The Park National Bank. Progress photographs of the construction.
From the Buckey family collection.

Left
Job 1230 The Park National Bank. Everett Reese turns the first shovel.
Photo from the Licking County Historical Society.

Licking Laundry had the Buckeys build a new building for them on Mt. Vernon Road. Opened there in 1957 was the Speedy Laundry, a new drive-in laundry and dry cleaners. The Jack Hemmer Ice Cream Shop occupied the south end of the building.

Holy Trinity Lutheran Church had their new Parish Hall dedicated in 1958. This new building provided classrooms, kitchen facilities and an all-purpose room in the two-story structure.

On January 21, 1959, the Licking River flooded large areas of Newark. All of the Buckey Brothers buildings had water inside and all residents on Riverside Drive were forced to evacuate. To reach the Buckey Brothers businesses, the Shackleford residence, and the Ohio Coal Company had to be driven past, thus one could not get to the Buckey buildings. Owens Corning Fiberglass, another neighbor of the Buckeys, was under eight feet of water.

The Rising River Association, also known as the River Rats, a social group of businessmen who had property damaged as a result of the flood, celebrated the first anniversary of the flood by installing a totem pole at the corner of Front Street and Everett Avenue to ward off future flooding. The chairman of the board of the Rising River Association was Stanley Brown, the president was Howard LeFevre, the secretory was R. E. Buckey, the vice president was Ed Galleher, and the treasurer was Frank Spencer

Above
The 1959 Flood, The Totem.
A clipping from the Magazine section of the Columbus Dispatch July 1962.

Sr. There were 19 members. Three new members were allowed to join each year if they could prove they were affected by the flood.

Left
The 1959 Flood, Shackleford residence on the corner of Sprague and Riverside Drive.
From the Buckey family collection.

Below
The 1959 Flood, Ohio Coal Company on the corner of Sprague and Riverside Drive.
From the Buckey family collection.

Left
The 1959 Flood, Some Rising River Association members. Left to Right: Robert Dawson, Robert Anderson, Stanley Brown, R. E. Buckey, G. E. Smith, Roy Crean, Ed Galleher, and Lynn Campbell.
A clipping from the Magazine section of the Columbus Dispatch July 1962.

In September of 1958, at 134 E. Locust Street, an addition was built to the Merchandising building. The flood of 1959 damaged their building and after flood threats in 1963 and 1964, Merchandising moved to 134 Everett Avenue. In 1965, a new building was built in Heath for Merchandising. Ownership then went from Ed Galleher to Ragal Corporation.

The Franklin Elementary School District and the Jacksontown School District merged in 1951 and became the Lynwood School District. In 1957, the Hebron and Lynwood School Districts then merged to form the Lakewood School District and the Davis farm on Route 40 became the location of the new Lakewood High School. The new school building was completed in 1959. The 5800-square-foot building was designed for 470 students and was expandable to accommodate 750students. At this time, the school was the only Licking County School to have a separate gymnasium and auditorium. The new Lakewood High School was dedicated March 20, 1960.

Above
Job 1296 Merchandising, Inc. Orville Varasso Architect's sketch.

A clipping from the Newark Advocate. From the Buckey family collection.

Below
Job 1313 Lakewood High School.

A clipping from the Newark Advocate. From the Buckey family collection.

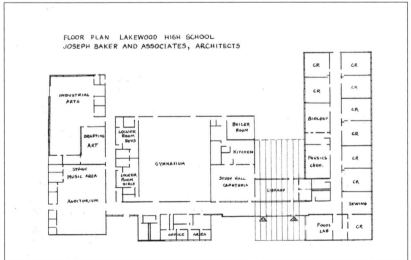

FLOOR PLAN LAKEWOOD HIGH SCHOOL
JOSEPH BAKER AND ASSOCIATES, ARCHITECTS

Left Top & Bottom
Job 1313 Lakewood High School.

Clippings from the Lakewood High School Dedication Program. From the Buckey family collection.

On April 1, 1959, First Federal Savings and Loan purchased the Park National Bank building at 32 N. Park Place. The interior 6,000 square feet was remodeled for the new owners by the Buckey Brothers. Extensive remodeling changed the entire appearance of the front of the building. The new contemporary design featured granite and metal grill work that gave a ribbed look with bronze risers from the sidewalk to the roof.

Below
Job 1380 The Park National Bank purchased by the First Federal Savings and Loan.
A 1959 photo from the Park National Bank.

Right
Job 1380 First Federal Savings and Loan. The new facade.
A clipping from the Newark Advocate. From the Buckey family collection.

FIRST FEDERAL SAVINGS

32 N. Park Place, Newark, Ohio

The fire at the Stewart Brothers and Alward Furniture Store in 1960 not only did structural damage to the first floor, but smoke damaged all of their sales areas, the furniture and their main office in the three-story building. Five other businesses in the west end of the Arcade suffered damage when the water poured on the burning roof seeped into their basements. Due to poor ventilation at the base of a chimney smokestack, heat from the basement boiler ignited the wood joists between the basement ceiling and the floor of the first story. Ambulances from local funeral homes were on standby since there was no Emergency Medical Services at this time. In July, the front on Church Street was remodeled and a canopy added.

Starting in July and completing October 1960, a Minit-Man Car Wash was built on East Church Street. One of the company's advertisements stated, *...it only takes a Minit to notice the difference.* The building was remodeled in 1968. (A picture of the building can be seen in the background of the Jim Grady Pontiac photo. Job 1450).

In December 1960, an early morning gas explosion at the National Gas and Oil Company on Granville Road damaged the rear of the building. It was determined that a defective steam safety valve malfunctioned and pressure built up in the boiler which caused it to explode. The front of the building was not damaged and as soon as temporary heat was restored, employees used the front entrance, only missing a day of work. The Buckeys rebuilt the three-year-old building after the explosion.

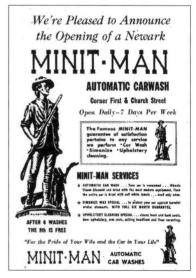

Above
Job1438-1 Stewart Brothers and Alward.

A clipping from the City Note Page of the Newark Advocate.

Left
Job 2036 Minit-Man Car Wash after the remodel.

Photo from the Buckey family collection.

Above
Job 1450 Minit-Man Car Wash.

Clippings from the City Note Page of the Newark Advocate.

1961-1965

FROM DR. A.D. PIATT TO SEAWAY DISCOUNT STORE

In 1961 at 36 West Church Street, Dr. A. D. Piatt installed a Cobalt-60 therapy unit, a new method for treating cancer. While remodeling his office, Buckey Brothers used 180 tons of specially treated concrete that went into the building to protect against radiation exposure. Some walls built were 50 inches thick.

Within John J. O'Neill's Southgate Shopping Center, Buckey Brothers built Rooms 25, 26, and 27 in 1961 and also followed with rooms 28, 29, and 30 in 1962.

In 1962, the Southgate Shopping Center had a gala opening for the new J. C. Penney store and sales were held in all of the stores

Includes New Penney Store

Plan $325,000 Southgate Addition

Left
Job 1577 Southgate Shopping Center. Surveying for groundbreaking at Southgate Shopping Center are, left to right, Richard Smith who will have another Casual Shop in one of the stores; Jack M. Maki, of Frank, Lindberg and Maki Architects, Columbus; Ernest Buckey of Buckey Brothers, Newark; Ron Prehm, Southgate Manager; and Lou Goodrich, Manager of J. C. Penney's Store which will move to the center when the new addition is finished.

A clipping from the Newark Advocate. From the Buckey family collection.

in the center. Locally this store was known as Penney's. Joining in the celebration along with Penney's were the Big Bear Super Market, Nash Women's Wear, The Southwind Lounge, TV Stamp Redemption Store, Park National Bank, Isaly's, Woolworth's, Alten's, Steppes Beauticians, Southgate Barbers, Monumental Life Insurance, Claggett and Quickel Insurance, City Loan, Riley's Bakery, W. T. Grant Company, Schiff's Shoes, Gray Drug Store, Southgate Hardware, Callander's Cleaners, Johnny's Southgate Carryout, the State Store, The Kroger Company, The Casual Shop and Pure Oil. The downtown Penney's store had around 20 employees, whereas the new Southgate Penney's had around 80 employees, with the average payroll per year of about $150,000.

In downtown Newark on Fourth Street, Licking Laundry was remodeled by the Buckey Brothers. Licking Laundry was founded in Newark in 1903 with two branches in Columbus and Lancaster.

Above

Job 1577 Southgate Shopping Center and Penney's Store.

A clipping from the Newark Advocate. From the Buckey family collection.

Below

Job 1586 Licking Laundry Services.

A clipping from the Newark Advocate.

Cosmo Investors, Inc., the property management company of Warren T. Suter, hired the Buckeys to remodel the fronts of the Mayfair Restaurant at 34 West Main Street, Elliott Hardware at 36 West Main Street, and the Newark Letter Shop at 38 West Main Street.

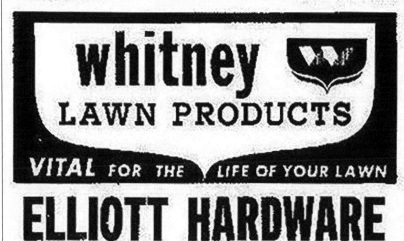

Above
Job 1606-1 Mayfair Restaurant.
A clipping from the Newark Advocate.

Left
Job 1606-2 Elliot Hardware.
A clipping from the Newark Advocate.

Left
Job 1606-3 Newark Letter Shop.
A clipping from the Newark Advocate.

During the winter of 1962, across from Southgate Shopping Center, Walker and Battat were celebrating the grand opening of their new Ford dealership which included a new sales area and repair building. Buckey Brothers chose all local subcontractors, and at the request of Bob Battat, local materials were used. The new structure provided better service in a less crowded building and at a lower cost to customers.

At 107-109 West Main Street, the brothers remodeled the building for Spencer-Walker Press, commercial printers, who had been located on three floors of the Advocate Building. Later, this building became the Newark High School band building.

Warren T. Suter's Cosmo Investors, Inc. hired the brothers to remodel the old Carousel Restaurant in the Schaus building on the east side of the square at 40 South First Street. This restaurant had been on the same site for ten years and was now to be known as The Carousel Supper Club, owned by the James Hays family. Seating increased from 175 to about 400 and the decor followed the carousel theme. Construction began in November 1963.

Developer John J. O'Neill's Southgate Development Corporation and the Park Union Corporation had both The Point Shopping Center (Southgate Corners Shopping Center) and Eastland Shopping Center under construction at the same time. They were started June 1964 and completed December 1964 by the Buckeys. The location for Eastland was the corner of Liberty Avenue and East Main Street in Newark. The stores located at the Eastland Shopping Center when they opened were Albers Grocery, Arcade Drug Store, Riley's Bakery and Luncheonette, Eastland Barbers, The M. Roberts Beauty Salon and the Eastland Laundry and Dry Cleaners. At the same time, Park National Bank built a branch on the east end of the center.

Below
Jobs 1850 and 1850 PNB
Eastland Shopping Center.
Photo from the Buckey family collection.

Bottom
Jobs 1850 and 1850 PNB
Eastland Shopping Center and
Park National Bank.
Advertising clipping from the Buckey family collection.

Left
Jobs 1850 and 1850 PNB
Eastland Shopping Center and
Park National Bank. William
Camp, Norwich, Ohio puts
in electrical wire at Eastland
Shopping Center. Workmen
from Holland Electric have
been roughing in the electrical
system for two days.

*A clipping from the Newark
Advocate. From the Buckey family
collection.*

Southgate Corners Shopping Center, also known as The Point
Shopping Center, was located at the corner of Route 79 and South
30th Street in Heath. Four stores and three county agriculture
offices occupied the 25,000-square-foot center with two stores
available for lease. The leased stores were Albers Grocery and
Norge Laundry City.

Left
Job 1860 Southgate Corners
Shopping Center.

*Photo from the Buckey family
collection.*

On the north side of the square where Gallaher Drugs had been located, the space was remodeled for McDonnell's Shoes. McDonnell's Shoes was founded in 1870 and since the early 1930s had been located at 24 South Second Street. The new store was completed in 1964.

In 1964, Newark Coca-Cola, which employed 26 people, was located in a back alley at 27 Arch Street, just off of East Main Street. There they bottled Coke, Tab, Sprite and orange, grape, root beer, cherry and cream sodas. They began to double the size of their existing bottling plant by tearing down six houses, a coal yard, along with garages and several sheds. This created space for the new 9,100-square-foot addition, along with a 160-square-foot lawn and a parking lot. According to Donn Alspach, sales manager, a bottling plant had been at this location since 1910. However, Coke had only been there since 1915.

Architect's sketch shows new Coca-Cola bottling plant as it will appear from East Main Street. Offices will be at left side of building. Windows in center will let outsiders peer into the plant area where soft drinks will be bottled. The building will be faced with white brick and red and white enamel panels. A 160-foot lawn will extend in front of the plant.

Left
Job 1881 Newark Coca-Cola.

A clipping from the Newark Advocate. From the Buckey family collection.

Coca-Cola Plant Rises

Left
Job 1881 Newark Coca-Cola. Coca-Cola's sales manager looks through the future site of a large window that will allow people to view the entire bottling process anytime during the day.

A clipping from the Newark Advocate. From the Buckey family collection.

Sherwin-Williams Paints store built a $40,000 one-floor new store on a site located in the same block as the Newark High School. Buckey Brothers completed the job in August 1965.

In 1965, G and R Realty built a 30,000-square-foot building east of Eastland Shopping Center for Seaway Discount Store. Robert Coffey, Seaway store owner, had opened the original Seaway on Everett Avenue in 1961. Later, a 5,000-foot garden center was added to the west end of the East Main Street Seaway store. Taking advantage of the new expressway, the owner coined the slogan Use the Freeway and Shop Seaway. An identical Seaway store was built by the Buckey Brothers in Washington Court House in 1967.

Below
Job 1900 Seaway Store Newark.
A clipping from the City Note Page of the Newark Advocate.

Artist's sketch shows new Seaway Discount Store to open this August at Eastland Shopping Center.

Above
Job 1900 Seaway Store Newark.

Photos from the Buckey family collection.

Left
Job 1900 Seaway Store Newark.

A clipping from the City Note Page of the Newark Advocate.

In 1966, Joseph Baker and Associates moved from their office at 180 Hudson Avenue to their new location on Sharon Valley Road. At this time, the firm had 20 employees.

In March of 1965, the office of Columbia Gas vacated their office on West Main Street to make room for the new City Hall. Their temporary office was located at 935 Buckeye Avenue. Buckey Brothers built their new division headquarters on West Church Street. The new building was designed with air conditioning powered by natural gas, and a drive-in payment window was provided on the east side of the building.

Left
Job 1911 Joseph Baker and Associates.
A clipping from the Newark Advocate. From the Buckey family collection.

Below
Job 1930 Columbia Gas Groundbreaking. Left to right: C. Allen Milliken, unknown, Eldon H. Davis, and R. E. Buckey.

Left
Job 1930 Columbia Gas Groundbreaking. Left to right: Everett Albyn, C. Allen Milliken, R. E Buckey, Eldon H. Davis, and J. V (Joy) Bishop.
Photos from the Buckey family collection.

1966-1970

FROM HOLY TRINITY LUTHERAN CHURCH TO STANDARD REGISTER

The last service in the sanctuary at Holy Trinity Lutheran Church was held March 20, 1966. The S. G. Lowendick Company bulldozed the old church that had been built in 1911. Buckey Brothers, who built the Parish Hall in 1958, (Job 1275), built the new Sanctuary, which now seats 340 people and is connected to the Parish Hall, also built by the Buckey Brothers.

Above & Below
Job 1945 Holy Trinity Lutheran Church.

Clippings from the Newark Advocate. From the Buckey family collection.

Architect's sketch shows new $100,000 stone and brick sanctuary of Holy Trinity Lutheran Church, corner Williams and West Main Streets.

The Egan Funeral home was being built at 141 North 24th Street. When completed, their previous location at the corner of W. Church and N. Fourth Streets was demolished for the construction of a new YWCA.

Funeral Home Nearly Done

Another addition to the growth of Newark's east end was the new Kentucky Fried Chicken carry-out at the Cedar Street exit off the new Route 16 Expressway.

Landscaping Sets Off Carry-Out

Left
Job 1950 The Egan Funeral Home.
A clipping from the Newark Advocate. From the Buckey family collection.

Left
Job 1955 Kentucky Fried Chicken.
A clipping from the Newark Advocate. From the Buckey family collection.

After three houses on First Street and two on Church Street were torn down, the Buckeys built an aluminum and red brick building to house offices, a showroom, and a customer lounge with a television area for Jim Grady. The new Jim Grady Pontiac building was 20,000 square feet in size. It was completed in September 1966 for the introduction of the 1967 Pontiac models.

Grady Pontiac Brightens Downtown

Jim Grady Pontiac's new showroom was one of the brighter additions to downtown Newark last year. The auto dealer also cleared several old houses at First and Church Streets for a display lot. (Advocate photo).

According to Timothy A. Clifford, president, Licking Laundry purchased a lot on West Main Street where a fire damaged an apartment building that was then demolished to make a new driveway to their Jefferson Street plant. The new driveway, south on West Main Street, was located immediately east of the bridge over Raccoon Creek.

Construction began on the new B. F. Goodrich Store in August of 1966. For 20 years, they had been located at 14 South Second Street and moved to make room for new wheel alignment and brake work areas. The service area increased six times from what they had at the old store. One-third of the 95,000-square-foot building would be for the sale of tires, refrigerators, freezers, radios, televisions, golf equipment, wheels, cameras, guns and ammunition. A separate warehouse addition to B. F. Goodrich was added in 1968.

Federal Mogul became the first tenant in John J. O'Neill's Newark Ohio Industrial Park. The Industrial Park was located on the former Eugene Hartshorn farm on Route 79 north of Hebron. The Detroit-based firm was one of the largest makers of bearings and manufactured a new gasket, Velcon, at this 24,000-square-foot plant that was completed in December 1967.

Above
Job 1965 B. F. Goodrich Store.

A clipping from the Newark Advocate. From the Buckey family collection.

In 1946, Howard LeFevere, founded B&L Motor Freight in Columbus, Ohio and moved it to Newark in 1947. It was the renowned trucking company from the 1940s until the 1970s. The Buckeys remodeled the office using Orville Varasso and Associates' plans.

Above
Job 2000 Federal Mogul.

A clipping from the Newark Advocate. From the Buckey family collection.

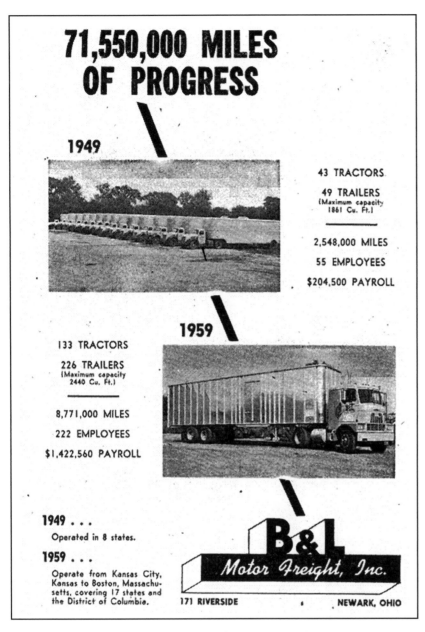

71,550,000 MILES OF PROGRESS

1949

43 TRACTORS

49 TRAILERS
(Maximum capacity 1861 Cu. Ft.)

2,548,000 MILES

55 EMPLOYEES

$204,500 PAYROLL

1959

133 TRACTORS

226 TRAILERS
(Maximum capacity 2440 Cu. Ft.)

8,771,000 MILES

222 EMPLOYEES

$1,422,560 PAYROLL

1949 . . .
Operated in 8 states.

1959 . . .
Operate from Kansas City, Kansas to Boston, Massachusetts, covering 17 states and the District of Columbia.

B&L Motor Freight, Inc.

171 RIVERSIDE • NEWARK, OHIO

Left
Job 1971 B&L Motor Freight.

A clipping from the Newark Advocate. From the Buckey family collection.

During July of 1968, after four years on the drawing board, Newark became the center of all Ohio National Guard Federal operations with the completion of the new Ohio National Guard Warehouse. The land where the warehouse was built was adjacent to the existing guard complex and had been donated by the Newark Area Chamber of Commerce. The one-story brick veneer building was used for storage and issuing of clothing. Upon completion of the warehouse, the former headquarters moved from Fort Hayes in Columbus to Licking County. Additions were added to the maintenance shop in 1970 by the Buckey Brothers.

At 132 West Church Street, the Egan Funeral Home was torn down for the construction of the YWCA. The new Y was planned in 1962; the funds acquired in 1965; and the grand opening was held, December, 1969. The building was originally planned for four stories with a swimming pool on the fourth floor. Since bids were higher than estimated, the plans were eventually revised to two stories. The pool of Olympic proportions was then located on the ground floor.

Below
Job 2020 YWCA. The two-story architect's sketch of the Church Street entrance of the YWCA.

A clipping from the Newark Advocate. From the Buckey family collection.

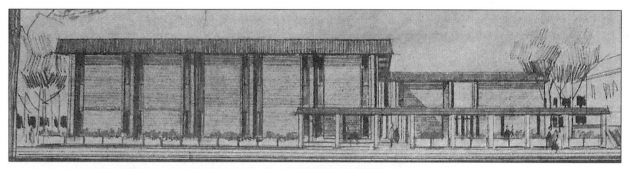

YWCA Building Construction Underway

Left
Job 2020 YWCA. Signing the construction contract, left to right, seated: Mrs. Willis Reese, R. E. Buckey, Contractor and Mrs. Ralph Woltjen, President of the YWCA Board of Directors. Back row: Darrel S. Jones, Gail Piper, Chairman of the Building Committee and Mrs. William C. Myers.

A clipping from the Ace News. From the Buckey family collection.

The Soldiers and Sailors Memorial Building, also known as the Auditorium Theater, was damaged by a fire on April 29, 1968. On April 30, the arsonist, a 20-year-old young man, was arrested. Movies scheduled in the Auditorium Theater were rescheduled when possible to the Midland Theatre. The seven members of the

Soldier and Sailors Board of Trustees hired the Buckey Brothers for the removal of the fire debris. Later it was decided to rebuild the first and second floors as far as the insurance monies would go.

Ground was broken, September, 1968 for the Dow Chemical Company's plant located in the Newark Ohio Industrial Park. The land, 125,000 acres, was purchased by Dow for the 75,000-square-foot building that employed 50 people. Trycite, a polystyrene film, would then be manufactured there. Trycite was a transparent material used for food wrapping, envelop windows, retail display and photographic film.

Above
Job 2040 Dow Chemical.
A clipping from the Newark Advocate. From the Buckey family collection.

Left
Job 2040 Dow Chemical.
A photograph showing the construction. From the Buckey family collection.

Bill Yost started his own chemical supply company in Newark. For the Wm. T. Yost Janitorial Supplies and Chemicals, an office and warehouse were remodeled in 1969 by the Buckey Brothers.

THIS IS THE HOUSE THAT DIRT BUILT

WE INVITE YOU TO VISIT OUR NEW SHOWROOM AND WAREHOUSE CONTAINING CENTRAL OHIO'S MOST COMPLETE LINE OF INDUSTRIAL AND COMMERCIAL CLEANING SUPPLIES AND EQUIPMENT.

WILLIAM T. YOST CO.

217 South 21st St.   344-9140

Left
Job 2053 William T. Yost Company.
A clipping from the Newark Advocate. From the Buckey family collection.

Fairfield Scientific Corporation moved into what was once the Kilgore Fireworks plant. Buckey Brothers completed a new production building in 1969 and followed with a new office building in 1970. Licking County purchased the real estate and the existing buildings by issuing tax-free bonds to cover the cost and to place monies into a construction fund. The plant was then leased back to Fairfield Scientific Corporation. This Granville site manufactured pyrotechnics and explosives for defense contracts. Employed there at this time were 200 people.

Below
Job 2050 Fairfield Scientific Corporation. Production Building.
A clipping from the Newark Advocate. From the Buckey family collection.

Left
Job 2060 Fairfield Scientific Corporation. Office Building and Machine Shop.
A clipping from the Newark Advocate. From the Buckey family collection.

National Hard Chrome Plating was the first company from outside the United States to become a tenant in the Newark Ohio Industrial Park. Their home offices were in Canada. The Buckeys built a twelve thousand square foot building for the company to manufacture high quality printing plates.

The American Legion purchased the former Cussins and Fearn building and remodeled it for their headquarters. Dedication of the new building for the American Legion Post #85 was held in the fall of 1970. This building had a full basement which housed Post and Unit offices, a club room and a kitchen. A ballroom on the ground floor was to be used for meetings and also for other public functions.

Left
Job 2062 American Legion Post 85.

A clipping from the Ohio Legion News. From the Buckey family collection.

Also in the Newark Ohio Industrial Park, Building #10, a 77,000-square-foot building was under construction. It was purchased by the Standard Register Corporation.

It was at this time, the Newark Advocate reported, *R. E. Buckey, president, announced February 4, 1971 that the firm, Buckey Brothers, would cease operations after completing the general contract for the Standard Register Company in the Newark Ohio Industrial Park, Hebron Road.*

Appendix I

Jobs in Alphabetical Order

NAME, OWNER, AGENT AND/OR BUSINESS	COMPLETED WORK	ADDRESS	JOB NUMBER	PAGE NUMBER
Adjutant General's Department, U.S.P. and F.O., State of Ohio	New Warehouse at the National Guard	1297 Hollar Lane	2010	73
Adjutant General's Department, U.S.P and F.O., State of Ohio	Additions to Combined Support and Maintenance Shop at the Newark Armory	1297 Hollar Lane	2070	73
Advocate Printing Company	Remodel the Advocate Store	25 W. Main Street	71	*
Advocate Printing Company	Addition to the Advocate Building	21-29 W. Main Street	502	*
American Legion Post #85	Remodel Cussins and Fearn for New American Legion Headquarters	58 E. Main Street	2062	77
American-Marietta Company	Addition to Booty Resineers	42 S. Third Street	1339	*
American-Marietta Company	Miscellaneous Work at Booty Resineers	42 S. Third Street	1520	*
Austin Company	Foundations and Floors at Balata Refining Company	1001 E. Main Street	1580	*
B and L Motor Freight, Inc.	Remodel the B and L Motor Freight Office	171 Riverside Drive	1971	72 and 73
Baker, Joseph	New Office Building	1000 Sharon Valley Road	1911	68
Batson Furniture Company, Market House	Remodel Market House	42 S. Second Street	1020	*

NAME, OWNER, AGENT AND/OR BUSINESS	COMPLETED WORK	ADDRESS	JOB NUMBER	PAGE NUMBER
Bennington Liberty Board of Education	Addition to Appleton School	6300 Von Fossen Road, Appleton	1188	*
Bishop Drive-In Restaurant, Emde, W. A.	New Bishop Drive-In Restaurant	856 Hebron Rd., Heath	1700	*
Buckey, R. E.	New Minit-Man Car Wash	100 E. Church Street	1450	58
Buckey, R.E.; Buckey, H.C.; Buckey, M.G.; and Buckey, E.W.	New A & P Super Market	34 S. Fifth Street	420	40
Buckey Realty Company	New A & P Super Market	205 S. Third Street, Coshocton	450	40
Burke Golf Company	Addition to Burke Golf Company Office	160 Essex Avenue	1363	*
Coca-Cola	Remodeling and Plant Addition for the Coca-Cola Plant	250 E. Main Street	1881	65
Columbia Gas of Ohio, Inc.	New Columbia Gas Office Building	135 W. Church Street	1930	68
Continental Can Company	Addition to Continental Can Plant on the South End	950 Brice St.	1650	*
Cornell Men's and Boy's Store	Remodel Cornell Store Front and Windows	24 N. Park Place	1390	*
Coshocton Board of Education	Addition to Union School	Rt. 79 Coshocton County	333	40
Coshocton Board of Education	New Farm Shop Building	*	370	40
Coshocton Board of Education	Addition to Lincoln School	801 Cambridge Road, Coshocton	435	40
Coshocton Board of Education	Addition to Sycamore School	Sycamore Street, Coshocton	436	40
Cosmo Investors, Inc.	Remodel a Storeroom	*	470	*
Cosmo Investors, Inc.	Remodel the Bazaar Building	24 N. Park Place	1370	*

NAME, OWNER, AGENT AND/OR BUSINESS	COMPLETED WORK	ADDRESS	JOB NUMBER	PAGE NUMBER
Cosmo Investors, Inc.	For the Addition to Industrial Automotive	595 W Church Street	1600	*
Cosmo Investors, Inc.	Remodel the Store Front for the Mayfair Restaurant	34 W. Main Street	1606-1	61
Cosmo Investors, Inc.	Remodel the Store Front for Elliot Hardware	36 W. Main Street	1606-2	61
Cosmo Investors, Inc.	Remodeling the Store Front for the Newark Letter Shop	38 W. Main Street	1606-3	61
Cosmo Investors, Inc., Carousel Restaurant	Remodel the Carousel Restaurant	40 S. First Street	1806	63
Curtis, Henry L.	Remodel the Curtis Hotel after a fire	6 Public Square, Mt. Vernon	40	*
Denison University	Repairs to College Town House after a fire	334 E. Broadway, Granville	830	43
Dog Pound	New Dog Pound Building	544 Dog Leg Road, Heath	187	35
Dow Chemical Corporation, Newark Ohio Industrial Park, Inc.	New Building #3, Dow Chemical Corporation, Trycite Plant	3700 Hebron Road, Newark Ohio Industrial Park, Hebron	2040	75
Dow Chemical Corporation, Newark Ohio Industrial Park, Inc.	Caisson Footings at Trycite Plant, Dow Chemical	3700 Hebron Road, Newark Ohio Industrial Park, Hebron	2044	*
Dow Chemical Corporation, Newark Ohio Industrial Park, Inc.	Process Structure and Foundations	3700 Hebron Road, Newark Ohio Industrial Park, Hebron	2048	*
Dow Chemical Corporation, Newark Ohio Industrial Park, Inc.	Saranex Enclosure at Trycite Plant, Dow Chemical	3700 Hebron Road, Newark Ohio Industrial Park, Hebron	2052	*
Dow Chemical Corporation, Newark Ohio Industrial Park, Inc.	Foundations for 12.5 KV Switchgear Building	3700 Hebron Road, Newark Ohio Industrial Park, Hebron	2071	*

NAME, OWNER, AGENT AND/OR BUSINESS	COMPLETED WORK	ADDRESS	JOB NUMBER	PAGE NUMBER
Eardly Lumber Company	Concrete and Masonry Work at Eardly Lumber Company	86 E. Locust Street	1291	*
Egan Funeral Home	New Egan Funeral Home	141 Green Wave Drive	1950	70
F. and A. M. Lodge #521	New Basement in Masonic Temple	Corner of E. Columbus Street and N. Church Street, Thornville	1658	77
Fairfield Scientific Corporation, Astro Fireworks Plant	Additions to Packing Building	2483 Dry Creek Road	2050	76
Fairfield Scientific Corporation, Astro Fireworks Plant	New Office Building and Machine Shop	2483 Dry Creek Road	2060	76
Federal Mogul Corporation, Newark Ohio Industrial Park, Inc.	New Building # 1, Federal Mogul	120 O'Neil Drive, Newark Ohio Industrial Park, Hebron	2000	72
Federal Mogul Corporation, Newark Ohio Industrial Park, Inc.	Hopper Pit, Walks, Fence, etc. at Federal Mogul	120 O'Neil Drive, Newark Ohio Industrial Park, Hebron	2000-X	*
Federal Mogul Corporation, Newark Ohio Industrial Park, Inc.	Foundations for 400,000 gallon Water Tank at Federal Mogul	120 O'Neil Drive SE, Newark Ohio Industrial Park, Hebron	2021	*
First Federal Savings and Loan	Remodel Park National Bank building for First Federal Savings and Loan	32 N. Park Place	1380	57
Flood of 1959			*	54 and 55
G and R Realty Company	Remodel Minit-Man Car Wash	100 E. Church Street	2036	58
Grady, Jim	New Jim Grady Pontiac Agency Sales Room	22 N. First Street	1960	71
Granville Board of Education	Addition to High School	310 N. Granger Street, Granville	433	*

NAME, OWNER, AGENT AND/OR BUSINESS	COMPLETED WORK	ADDRESS	JOB NUMBER	PAGE NUMBER
Granville Board of Education	Addition to Granville Elementary School	310 N. Granger Street, Granville	999	*
Granville Board of Education	Sewage System at Union School	745 Union Station Road, Granville	1326	*
Heath Local School District Board of Education	New Fulton School Bus Garage	160 Heath Road, Heath	1205	41
Hines Distributing Company	New Warehouse	111 S. Twenty First Street	1550	*
Holophane Company, Inc.	New Engineering Building	214 Oakwood Avenue	740	*
Holophane Company, Inc.	Tank Building and Miscellaneous Work at Holophane	214 Oakwood Avenue	1117	*
Holophane Company, Inc.	Addition to Research Engineering Center	214 Oakwood Avenue	1750	*
Holy Trinity Lutheran Church	Addition to Holy Trinity Lutheran Church	592 W. Main Street	1275	54
Holy Trinity Lutheran Church	New Sanctuary Unit	592 W. Main Street	1945	69
Huffman Motor Sales	New Huffman Motor Sales	675 W. Church Street	3	*
Jacksontown Board of Education	Addition to Jacksontown School	9100 Jacksontown Road, Jacksontown	855	44
Jeffers Brothers	Remodel Jeffers Brothers Store Fronts	45-47 S. Third Street	1864	*
John, Johnny	Addition to Cherry Valley Laundry	29 S. Twenty-ninth Street	1563	*
Kaiser Aluminum Company, Permante Metals	New Machine Foundations, etc.	600 Kaiser Drive, Heath	281 & Various Jobs	37

NAME, OWNER, AGENT AND/OR BUSINESS	COMPLETED WORK	ADDRESS	JOB NUMBER	PAGE NUMBER
Kaiser Aluminum Company	New Machinery Foundations	600 Kaiser Drive, Heath	371	37
Kaiser Aluminum Company, Various Jobs	Total Miscellaneous Jobs for 1951	600 Kaiser Dr. Heath	Shown after job 520	*
Kaydan, Inc., Industrial Automotive	Remodel Offices of Industrial Automotive	595 W. Church Street	2022	*
Kentucky Fried Chicken	New Kentucky Fried Chicken Take Home Store	38 N. Cedar Street	1955	70
King's Department Store, Eli Hull, Estate c/o George McDonald	Remodel after Fire at King's Department Store for Bargain Shoes	15 N. Third Street	1755	*
King's Department Store, Hull, Eli Estate c/o George McDonald	Remodel at King's Department Store for Bargain Shoe Store	15 N. Third Street	2002	*
Kress Box Company	New Concrete Floor at Kress Box Company	205 S. Twenty-first Street	426	*
Kress Box Company	New Office Building at Kress Box Company	205 S. Twenty-first Street	514	*
Kress Box Company, Trimble Company	Plant Addition at Kress Box Company	205 S. Twenty First Street	660	*
Lakewood Board of Education	New Building for Lakewood High School	5222 National Road, Hebron	1313	56
Licking Laundry	New Building for Jack Hemmer and Speedy Laundry Cleaners	340 Mt. Vernon Road	1240	54
Licking Laundry	Remodel Licking Laundry Services Building	29 N. Fourth Street	1586	60
Licking Laundry Company Inc.	Plant Addition for Licking Laundry General Office	76 Jefferson Street	1963	71

NAME, OWNER, AGENT AND/OR BUSINESS	COMPLETED WORK	ADDRESS	JOB NUMBER	PAGE NUMBER
Licking Valley Local School District Board of Education	Addition to Perry School	4661 Licking Valley Road	1220	*
Lustron House	Prefabricated Home	381 N. Twenty-first Street	282	38
McDonnell's Shoe Store	Remodel for New McDonnell's Shoe Store	26 N. Park Place	1870	65
McKean Township Board of Education	Addition to McKean School	6151 State Rt. 661, Fredonia	520	*
Madison Township Board of Education	Addition to Madison School	1717 E. Main Street	1080	*
Med-O-Pure Dairy, Washington Court House	Dairy Building	1024 Leesburg Avenue, Washington Court House	777	42
Med-O-Pure Dairy, Washington Court House, Buckey Realty Company	Addition to Dairy Building	1024 Leesburg Avenue, Washington Court House	1003	42
Med-O-Pure Dairy, Washington Court House, Buckey Realty Company	Addition to Dairy Building	1024 Leesburg Avenue, Washington Court House	1441	42
Merchandising, Buckey R. E.	Addition to the Merchandising Building	134 E. Locust Street	1296	56
Merchandising, Ragal Corporation	New Building for Merchandising	585 Industrial Parkway, Heath	1901	56
Missionaries of Saints Peter and Paul	New Seminary Building at the Wehrle Farm	2734 Seminary Road, Heath	1177	50 and 51
Mitchell, Dr. Louis A.	Firestone Store	80 N. Third Street	1040	47
National Hard Chrome Plating, Newark Ohio Industrial Park, Inc.	New Building #5, National Hard Chrome Plating	141 Milliken Drive, Newark Ohio Industrial Park, Hebron	2055	77

NAME, OWNER, AGENT AND/OR BUSINESS	COMPLETED WORK	ADDRESS	JOB NUMBER	PAGE NUMBER
National Gas and Oil Company	Rebuild National Gas and Oil Building after Explosion	1500 Granville Road	1522	58
Neal Avenue Methodist Church	Remodel the Dining Room and Kitchen	12 Neal Avenue	1993	*
Newark Advocate Company, WCLT Radio Station	New Radio Station, WCLT	674 Jacksontown Road, Heath	1	31
Newark Baseball Company	New Baseball Park named Arnold Park	470 W. Church Street	79	30 and 31
Newark Board of Education	New Benjamin Franklin Junior High School	533 Beacon Road	940	45
Newark Board of Education	New Sidewalks and Curbs at Benjamin Franklin Junior High School	533 Beacon Road	1087	45
Newark Board of Education	Repair Roof at Cherry Valley Elementary School	1040 W. Main Street	1938	*
Newark Meat Supply	New Addition to Building and Remodeling	155 Clinton Street	2063	*
Newark Processing Company, Inc.	New Concrete Sludge Tank	160 Everett Avenue	1717	*
Newark Processing Company, Inc.	Concrete Slab Around Building	160 Everett Avenue	1928	*
Newark Township Board of Education	Addition to Newark Township School	300 Deo Drive	335	41
Newark Township Board of Education	Remodel Newark Township School	300 Deo Drive	410	41
Newark Township Board of Education	New Fulton School Gymnasium and Auditorium	160 Heath Road, Heath	440	41
Newark Township Board of Education	Addition to North Elementary School	300 Deo Drive	840	41

NAME, OWNER, AGENT AND/OR BUSINESS	COMPLETED WORK	ADDRESS	JOB NUMBER	PAGE NUMBER
Newark Township Board of Education	Addition to Fulton School	160 Heath Road, Heath	860	41
Newark Township Trustees	New #2 Fire Station Building	310 Deo Drive	610	*
Owens Corning Fiberglass Corporation	New Compressor Building	400 Case Avenue	472	*
Owens Corning Fiberglass Corporation Various Jobs	Total Miscellaneous Jobs for Year 1951 Exclusive of Job #472	400 Case Avenue	*	*
Owens Corning Fiberglass Corporation Various Jobs	Total Miscellaneous Jobs for 1953	400 Case Avenue	*	*
Owens Corning Fiberglass Corporation Various Jobs	Total Miscellaneous Jobs for Year 1954	400 Case Avenue	*	*
Owens Corning Fiberglass Corporation, Drake and Townsend	New Propane Plant	400 Case Avenue	509	*
Owens Corning Fiberglass, Kaighin and Hughes, Inc.	Construction work for Kaighin and Hughes at Owens Corning Fiberglass	400 Case Avenue	925-936-950	*
Owens Corning Fiberglass Corporation	New Conveyor Pit	400 Case Avenue	1030	*
Owens Corning Fiberglass Corporation	Remodel Building #39	400 Case Avenue	1540	*
Owens Corning Fiberglass Corporation	Phase II Office Consolidation for Building #41	400 Case Avenue	1616	*

NAME, OWNER, AGENT AND/OR BUSINESS	COMPLETED WORK	ADDRESS	JOB NUMBER	PAGE NUMBER
Owens Corning Fiberglass Corporation, Lieb-Jackson, Inc.	New Owens Corning Fiberglass Recirculating Plant	400 Case Avenue	1770	*
Owens Corning Fiberglass Corporation	Repair Hydraulic Lift Bridge	400 Case Avenue	1777	*
Owens Corning Fiberglass Corporation	New Foundation and Trench for Building #11	400 Case Avenue	1818	*
Owens Corning Fiberglass Corporation	Modifications in Buildings #7 and #41	400 Case Avenue	1840 (A-B-C-D-E-F)	*
Owens Corning Fiberglass Corporation	Remodel in Building #27	400 Case Avenue	1863 A&B	*
Owens Corning Fiberglass Corporation	Construct Wall in Building #26	400 Case Avenue	1919	*
Park National Bank	Remodel Schiff Shoe Store	31 S. Park Place	1150	*
Park National Bank	New Park National Bank Building	50 N. Third Street	1230	53
Park National Bank	New Park National Bank Branch in Eastland Shopping Center	1008 E. Main Street	1850 PNB	63
Park National Bank	Remodel Second Floor for the Park National Bank Trust Department	50 N. Third Street	2039	53
Park Union Corporation	New Eastland Shopping Center	986-998 E. Main Street	1850	63 and 64
Piatt, Dr. A. D.	New X-ray Room in Doctor's Office	36 W. Locust Street	1566	59
Postal Printing Company	New Postal Printing Office Supply Store	15 N. Fourth Street	832	43
Powell Electric	Remodel Powell Electric Building	31 N. Fifth Street	169	34
Production Built Homes	Foundations and Chimney Work on Fifty Homes	S. Thirty-Fourth Street	81-81A-105	34

NAME, OWNER, AGENT AND/OR BUSINESS	COMPLETED WORK	ADDRESS	JOB NUMBER	PAGE NUMBER
Public Finance Company, Arcade Realty	Remodel Public Finance Office	29 N. Third Street	2012	*
Pure Oil Company	Remodel Gas Station	*	399	*
Pure Oil Company	New Wash Bay addition	411 Union Street	1676	*
Reinhard, Walter	New Laundry Building	*	1555	*
Rockwell-Standard Corporation	Concrete Apron in Storage Area	444 Hebron Road	1628	*
Rockwell-Standard Corporation	Remodel Waiting Room Office	444 Hebron Road	1771	*
St. Edwards Catholic Church, Catholic Diocese of Columbus	New St. Edwards Catholic Church	785 Newark Granville Road, Granville	960	46
St. Edwards Catholic Church, Catholic Diocese of Columbus	New Rectory and Common Rooms	785 Newark Granville Road, Granville	1085	46
St. Francis de Sales Catholic Church	New School Gymnasium	20 Pearl Street	340	39
St. John's Evangelical Church	Addition to Church	285 W. National Drive	1155	48 and 49
Seaboard Finance Company, Emde, W. A.	New Store Front at Seaboard Finance	11 W. Main Street	1642	*
Sears Building, Thirty-Three West Main Corporation	Remodel Sears Building	33 W. Main Street	1990	*
Seaway Store, G and R Realty Company	New Seaway Store in Newark	1058 E. Main Street	1900	66 and 67
Seaway Store, G and R Realty Company	New Seaway Store in Washington Court House	CCC Highway-W, Washington Court House	1991	66

NAME, OWNER, AGENT AND/OR BUSINESS	COMPLETED WORK	ADDRESS	JOB NUMBER	PAGE NUMBER
Second Presbyterian Church	Addition to Sunday School Building	42 E. Church Street	1013	*
Self Serve Food Market, Buckey Realty Company	New Self Serve Food Market	110 Cemetery Road, Hilliard	1620	*
Sherwin Williams Company, James O. Austin	New Sherwin Williams Paint Store	140 W. Main Street	1898	66
Slayter, Games	Addition to Residence	7720 White Chapel Road	478	41
Smyth Manufacturing Company	New Warehouse Building	25 Forry Avenue	1516	*
Soldiers and Sailors Memorial Building, Auditorium	Removing Fire Debris at the Auditorium Building	22 N Third Street	2035	74 and 75
Southgate Development Corporation	New Southgate Corners Shopping Center	793-811 Hebron Road, Heath	1860	63 and 64
Southgate Shopping Center, Penney's	New Penney's Store, Rooms 25, 26, 27	553-635 Hebron Road, Heath	1577	59 and 60
Southgate Shopping Center Corporation	Rooms 28, 29, and 30, New Additions	553-635 Hebron Road, Hebron	1660	59
Spalding, R. M.	New Spalding Farm Center Building	600 W. Church Street	4	*
Spencer Walker Press	Remodel Spencer Walker Press Building	107 W. Main Street	1686	62
Standard Register, Newark Ohio Industrial Park, Inc.	New Building #10, Standard Register	190 Milliken Drive SE Newark Ohio Industrial Park, Hebron	2080	77
State of Ohio	New Laundry Building at the State Hospital, Mt. Vernon	Rian Road, Mt. Vernon	120	*
Stewart Brothers and Alward Company, Arcade Realty	Remodel after a Fire	21-27 West Church Street	1438	58

NAME, OWNER, AGENT AND/OR BUSINESS	COMPLETED WORK	ADDRESS	JOB NUMBER	PAGE NUMBER
Stewart Brothers and Alward Company, Arcade Realty	Remodel Church Street Front and Canopy	21-27 West Church Street	1444	58
Taylor, Josephine	Remodel Store Front for City Drug Store	12 N. Park Place	1431-1	*
Taylor, Josephine	Remodel Store Front for Natoma Restaurant	10 N. Park Place	1431-2	*
Tectum Corporation	New Tectum Plant Building	105 S. Sixth Street	367	*
Tectum Corporation	New Concrete Floors and Remodel Building	105 S. Sixth St.	368-382-384-389-390-391-393-394-407-414	*
Tectum Corporation	Addition to Picker Room	105 S. Sixth St.	1640	*
Texaco Gas Station, Buckey, R. E.	New Texaco Gas Station	W. Church Street and Granville Road	1180	52
Upham, S. P., Kroger Store	Remodel Kroger Store	74 S. Second Street	188	*
Utica - Washington Board of Education	New Elementary School	Corner of Spring Street and Washington Street	240	36
Van Voorhis, Robert F.	Addition to City Loan Office	18 S. Second Street	1383	*
Vercoe and Company	Remodel New East Church Street Vercoe and Company Office	21 E. Church Street	2034	*
Walker, Raymond and Battat, Robert	New Building for Auto Sales and Repairs	500 Hebron Road, Heath	1630	62
Walker, Raymond and Battat, Robert, B.F. Goodrich	New Store for B.F. Goodrich	510 Hebron Road, Heath	1965	72

NAME, OWNER, AGENT AND/OR BUSINESS	COMPLETED WORK	ADDRESS	JOB NUMBER	PAGE NUMBER
Walker, Raymond and Battat, Robert, B.F. Goodrich	Warehouse Additon to B.F. Goodrich Store	433 Hopewell Drive, Heath	2030	*
W.C.L.T., Inc.	Addition to WCLT Radio Station	674 Jacksontown Road, Heath	1970	31
Weiss, Lawrence A.	Addition to Larry's Drug Store	350 E. Main Street	1560	*
Westhall Company	Remodel Hub Store for Mills Drugs	7 N. Third Street	1925	*
Westinghouse Electric	Remodel Westinghouse Plant	325-327 W. Main Street	613	*
Westinghouse Electric	Remodel Westinghouse Plant	325-327 W. Main Street	628	*
Y.M.C.A.	New Bathhouse at the Pool	470 W. Church Street	1740	*
Y.W.C.A. of Licking County	New Building and Indoor Pool	Corner of W. Church Street and N. Sixth St.	2020	74
Yost, William T. Company	New Office and Warehouse	217 S. Twenty First Street	2053	76

* Information not Available

Appendix II

Jobs in the Order they Were Built

JOB NUMBER	NAME, OWNER, AGENT AND/OR BUSINESS	ARCHITECT	BUILDING	MONTH/ YEAR(S) BUILT	COST
1	Newark Advocate Company	Sims, Cornelius and Schooley	Radio Station	03/1946-07/1947	$48,249
3	Huffman Motor Sales	D. A. Carmichael	Motor Sales	03/1946-11/1947	$49,764
4	Spalding, R. M.	D. A. Carmichael	Farm Center	03/1946-07/1947	$51,089
40	Curtis, Henry L.	Herbert S. Jones	Curtis Hotel, Mt. Vernon	08/1946-03/1947	$80,163
71	Advocate Printing Company		Advocate Store	01/1947-10/1947	$17,863
79	Newark Baseball Company		Arnold Park	03/1947-08/1947	$19,491
81-81A, 105	Production Built Homes		Housing Project	04/1947-10/1947	$38,792
120	State of Ohio	Joseph A. Gattozzi	State Hospital, Mt. Vernon	09/1947-12/1947	$143,256
169	Powell Electric		Powell Electric Building	12/1947-02/1948	*
187	Dog Pound		Dog Pound	04/1948-10/1948	*
188	Upham, S. P., Kroger Store		Kroger Store	07/1948-11/1948	$15,165
240	Utica-Washington Board of Education	T. D. McLaughlin and J. J. Keil	Elementary School	08/1948-08/1949	$129,885
281 and Various Jobs	Kaiser Aluminum, Permanente Metals	Plant Constructors	Kaiser Aluminum	12/1948-06/1949	$66,110

JOB NUMBER	NAME, OWNER, AGENT AND/OR BUSINESS	ARCHITECT	BUILDING	MONTH/ YEAR(S) BUILT	COST
282	Lustron House		Prefabricated Home	*-03/1949	*
333	Coshocton Board of Education	Fred D. Jacobs	Union School	06/1949-12/1949	$34,232
335	Newark Township Board of Education	Vernon Redding and Associates	Newark Township School	07/1949-01/1950	$21,475
340	St. Francis de Sales Catholic Church	Sims, Cornelius and Schooley	Gymnasium	06/1949-05/1950	$133,988
367	Tectum Corporation		Tectum Building	01/1950-02/1950	$16,348
370	Coshocton Board of Education	Fred D. Jacobs	Farm Shop Building	02/1950-06/1950	$15,955
371	Kaiser Aluminum Company		Machinery Foundations	01/1950-02/1950	$5,380
368, 382, 384, 389, 390, 391, 393, 394, 407, 414	Tectum Corporation		Tectum Building	01/1950-06/1950	$32,263
399	Pure Oil Company		Gas Station	05/1950-07/1950	$6,252
410	Newark Township, Board of Education	Joseph E. Baker	Newark Township School	06/1950-08/1950	$14,298
420	Buckey, R. E.; Buckey, H. C.; Buckey, M. G., and Buckey, E. W.		A & P Super Market	07/1950-11/1950	$66,500
426	Kress Box Company	Kress Box Company	Kress Box Company	08/1950-08/1950	$6,750
433	Granville Board of Education	T. D. McLaughlin and J. J. Keil	Granville High School	08/1950-08/1951	$35,353
435	Coshocton Board of Education	Fred D. Jacobs	Lincoln School	08/1950-10/1951	$70,958

JOB NUMBER	NAME, OWNER, AGENT AND/OR BUSINESS	ARCHITECT	BUILDING	MONTH/ YEAR(S) BUILT	COST
436	Coshocton Board of Education	Fred D. Jacobs	Sycamore School	08/1950-10/1951	$41,273
440	Newark Township Board of Education	Joseph E. Baker	Fulton School	08/1950-10/1951	$93,033
450	Buckey Realty Company		A & P Super Market, Coshocton	01/1951-08/1951	$51,516
470	Cosmo Investors, Inc.	Joseph E. Baker	Storeroom	12/1950-07/1951	$36,222
472	Owens Corning Fiberglass Corporation		Compressor Building	02/1951-11/1951	$29,811
478	Slayter, Games	Sims, Cornelius and Schooley	Residence	02/1951-09/1951	$43, 004
502	Advocate Printing Company		Advocate Building	05/1951-10/1951	$11,950
509	Owens Corning Fiberglass Corporation, Drake and Townsend		Owens Corning Fiberglass Propane Plant	05/1951-12/1951	$18,628
514	Kress Box Company		Office	07/1951-10/1951	$16,960
520	McKean Township Board of Education	T. D. McLaughlin and J. J. Keil	McKean School	08/1951-03/1952	$44,848
Total Misc. Jobs for Year 1951	Owens Corning Fiberglass Corporation		Exclusive of Job #472	01/1951-12/1951	$38,752
Total Misc. Jobs for 1951	Kaiser Aluminum Company		Various Jobs	01/1951-12/1951	$32,484
610	Newark Township Trustees	Joseph E. Baker	Fire Station	02/1952-06/1952	$16,782

JOB NUMBER	NAME, OWNER, AGENT AND/OR BUSINESS	ARCHITECT	BUILDING	MONTH/ YEAR(S) BUILT	COST
613	Westinghouse Electric Company		Westinghouse Plant	03/1952-04/1952	$10,748
628	Westinghouse Electric Company		Westinghouse Plant	03/1952-04/1952	$6,061
660	Kress Box Company, Trimble Company		Kress Box Company	07/1952-12/1952	$18,155
740	Holophane Company, Inc.	Sims, Cornelius and Schooley	Engineering Building	10/1952-05/1953	$79,089
777	Med-O-Pure Dairy, Washington Court House, Buckey Realty Company		Dairy Building, Washington Court House	12/1952-08/1953	$99,586
830	Denison University		College Town House, Granville	04/1953-06/1953	$19, 889
832	Postal Printing Company		Postal Printing Office Supply Store	04/1953-08/1953	$21,000
840	Newark Township Board of Education	Joseph E. Baker	North Elementary School	06/1953-02/1954	$87,471
855	Jacksontown Board of Education	Joseph E. Baker	Jacksontown School	07/1953-02/1954	$62,211
860	Newark Township Board of Education	Joseph E. Baker	Fulton School	10/1953-05/1954	$45,190
Total Misc. Jobs for 1953	Owens Corning Fiberglass Corporation			01/1953-12/1953	$37,900
925, 936, 950	Owens Corning Fiberglass, Kaighin and Hughes, Inc.		Owens Corning Fiberglass	03/1954-07/1954	$26,515
940	Newark Board of Education	Joseph E. Baker	Benjamin Franklin Junior High School	03/1954-07/1955	$311,725
960	St. Edwards Catholic Church, Catholic Diocese of Columbus	Johnson and Boutin and Walter Litwin, Associates	St. Edwards Catholic Church	05/1954-03/1955	$64,685

JOB NUMBER	NAME, OWNER, AGENT AND/OR BUSINESS	ARCHITECT	BUILDING	MONTH/ YEAR(S) BUILT	COST
999	Granville Board of Education	T. D. McLaughlin and J. J. Keil	Granville Elementary School	08/1954-09/1955	$120,127
Total Misc. for 1954	Owens-Corning Fiberglass Corporation			01/1954-12/1954	$31,972
1003	Med-O-Pure Dairy, Washington Court House, Buckey Realty Company		Med-O-Pure Dairy, Washington Court House	10/1954-12/1954	$13,093
1013	Second Presbyterian Church		Sunday School Building	10/1954-02/1955	$34,944
1020	Batson Furniture Company, Market House		Market House	12/1954-01/1955	$13,794
1030	Owens Corning Fiberglass Corporation		Conveyor Pit	02/1955-03/1955	$17,893
1040	Mitchell, Dr. Louis A.		Firestone Store	02/1955-09/1955	$50,899
1080	Madison Township Board of Education	Merle Orr	Madison School	07/1955-09/1956	$94,616
1085	St. Edwards Catholic Church, Catholic Diocese of Columbus	Walter Litwin	St. Edwards Catholic Church	07/1955-03/1956	$67,527
1087	Newark Board of Education	Joseph E. Baker	Benjamin Franklin Junior High School	07/1955-09/1955	$13,772
1117	Holophane Company, Inc.		Tank Building	12/1955-01/1956	$13,152
1150	Park National Bank	Joseph E. Baker	Shoe Store	01/1956-04/1956	$34,321
1155	St. John's Evangelical Church	Ralph R. Orr	St. John's Evangelical Church	03/1956-03/1957	$145,848
1177	Missionaries of Sts. Peter and Paul	Victor J. Basso	Saints Peter and Paul Seminary	05/1956-12/1956	$254,187
1180	Texaco Gas Station, Buckey, R. E.		Gas Station	05/1956-12/1956	$18,000
1188	Bennington Liberty Board of Education	Joseph E. Baker	Appleton School	05/1956-01/1957	$63,672

JOB NUMBER	NAME, OWNER, AGENT AND/OR BUSINESS	ARCHITECT	BUILDING	MONTH/YEAR(S) BUILT	COST
1205	Heath Local School District Board of Education	Joseph E. Baker	Bus Garage	07/1956-12/1956	$27,835
1220	Licking Valley Local School District Board of Education	Joseph E. Baker	Perry School	02/1957-08/1958	$32,853
1230	Park National Bank	Joseph E. Baker	Park National Bank	02/1957-05/1958	$591,860
1240	Licking Laundry	Sims, Cornelius and Schooley	Jack Hemmer and Speedy Laundry	05/1957-08/1957	$34,007
1275	Holy Trinity Lutheran Church	Frederick Stritzel	Holy Trinity Lutheran Church	03/1958-11/1958	$87,807
1291	Eardley Lumber Company		Eardly Lumber Company	05/1958-09/195	$18,478
1296	Merchandising, Buckey, R. E.		Merchandising	06/1958-09/1958	$14,419
1313	Lakewood Board of Education	Joseph E. Baker	Lakewood High School	09/1958-11/1959	$427,324
1326	Granville Board of Education	McLaughlin and Keil	Union School	11/1958-04/1959	$10,075
1339	American-Marietta Company	Themselves	Booty Resineers	03/1959-05/1959	$22,022
1363	Burke Golf Company	Orville Varasso	Office	07/1959-11/1959	$29,708
1370	Cosmo Investors, Inc.	William Kramer	The Bazaar	07/1959-12/1959	$24,065
1380	First Federal Savings and Loan	Joseph E. Baker	Park National Bank	08/1959-03/1960	$69,963
1383	Van Voorhis, Robert F.		City Loan	09/1959-11/1959	$10,829
1390	Cornell Men's and Boy's Store		Cornell Men's and Boy's Store	10/1959-12/1959	$9,369
1431-1	Taylor, Josephine		City Drug Store	03/1960-04/1960	$7,970 for 1 and 2

JOB NUMBER	NAME, OWNER, AGENT AND/OR BUSINESS	ARCHITECT	BUILDING	MONTH/ YEAR(S) BUILT	COST
1431-2	Taylor, Josephine		Natoma Restaurant	03/1960-04/1960	see above
1438	Stewart Brothers and Alward Company, Arcade Realty		Stewart Brothers and Alward	03/1960-06/1960	$17,826
1441	Med-O-Pure Dairy, Washington Court House, Buckey Realty Company		Med-O-Pure Dairy, Washington Court House	03/1960-08/1960	$15,824
1444	Stewart Brothers and Alward Company, Arcade Realty		Stewart Brothers and Alward	06/1960-07/1960	$15,000
1450	Buckey, Robert E.		Minit-Man Car Wash	07/1960-10/1960	$20,979
1516	Smyth Manufacturing Company		Smyth Warehouse	11/1960-03/1961	$29,080
1520	American-Marietta Company		Booty Resineers	12/1960-03/-1961	$9,975
1522	National Gas and Oil Company	Orville Varasso	National Gas and Oil Building	12/1960-09/1961	$51,218
1540	Owens-Corning Fiberglass Corporation	Themselves	Building No. #39	04/1961-10/1961	$170,248
1550	Hines Distributing		New Warehouse	05/1961-08/1961	$80,616
1555	Reinhard, Walter.		Laundry	06/1961-09/1961	$16,805
1560	Weiss, Lawrence A.	Blum and Jamison	Larry's Drug Store	08/1961-12/1961	$19,149
1563	John, Johnny		Cherry Valley Laundry	07/1961-08/1961	$5,022
1566	Piatt, Dr. A. D.		Doctor's Office	07/1961-12/1961	$9,406
1577	Southgate Shopping Center, Penney's	Frank, Lindberg and Maki	Penny's Store	09/1961-04/1962	$320,351
1580	Austin Company	Austin Company	Balate Refining	09/1961-11/1961	$5,8038
1586	Licking Laundry Company		Licking Laundry Services	10/1961-01/1962	$11,915
1600	Cosmo Investors, Inc.	William Kramer	Industrial Automotive	03/1962-05/1962	$21,700

JOB NUMBER	NAME, OWNER, AGENT AND/OR BUSINESS	ARCHITECT	BUILDING	MONTH/ YEAR(S) BUILT	COST
1606-1	Cosmo Investors, Inc.	William Kramer	Mayfair Restaurant	03/1962-05/1962	$5,951 for all 1606 jobs
1606-2	Cosmo Investors, Inc.	William Kramer	Elliot Hardware	03/1962-05/1962	(see above)
1606 -3	Cosmo Investors, Inc.	William Kramer	Newark Letter Shop	03/1962-05/1962	(see above)
1616	Owens Corning Fiberglass Corporation	Themselves	Building #41	04/1962-10/1962	$142,750
1620	Self Serve Food Market, Buckey Realty Company	Orville Varasso	New Food Market, Hilliard	06/1962-09/1962	$30.000
1628	Rockwell-Standard Corporation	Themselves	Storage Area	05/1962-06/1962	$14,385
1630	Walker, Raymond and Battat, Robert	Joseph Baker and Associates	Walker and Battat Ford	05/1962-12/1962	$222,445
1640	Tectum Corporation		Picker Room	06/1962-08/1962	$5,335
1642	Seaboard Finance, Emde, W. A.		Seaboard Finance	06/1962-08/1962	$5,073
1650	Continental Can Company	Varo Engineers	Continental Can Company	08/1962-10/1962	$19,082
1658	F. & A. M. Lodge #521	Blum, Jamison and Maki	Masonic Temple	09/1962-10/1962	$11,857
1660	Southgate Shopping Center Corporation	Frank, Lindberg and Maki	Shopping Center	09/1962-11/1962	$37,115
1676	Pure Oil Company	Themselves	Gas Station	10/1962-12/1962	$6,338
1686	Spencer Walker Press	Orville Varasso	Spencer-Walker Press	11/1962-06/1963	$18,041
1700	Bishop Drive-In Restaurant, Emde, W. A.	M. Bishop Plant	Bishop Drive-In Restaurant	04/1963-06/1963	$30,894
1717	Newark Processing Company, Inc.		Sludge Tank	05/1963-06/1963	$9,361

JOB NUMBER	NAME, OWNER, AGENT AND/OR BUSINESS	ARCHITECT	BUILDING	MONTH/ YEAR(S) BUILT	COST
1740	YMCA Family Park and Pool	Joseph Baker and Associates	Bathhouse	05/1963-06/1963	$19,705
1750	Holophane Company, Inc.	Sims, Cornelius and Schooley	Research Engineering Center	06/1963-12/1963	$86,984
1755	King's Department Store, Eli Hull Estate		King's Department Store	06/1963-11/1963	$63,839
1770	Owens Corning Fiberglass Corporation, Lieb-Jackson, Inc.	Owens Corning Fiberglass	Recirculating Plant	07/1963-11/1963	$51,000
1771	Rockwell-Standard Corporation	Themselves	Office	08/1963-09/1963	$12,995
1777	Owens Corning Fiberglass Corporation	Themselves	Hydraulic Lift Bridge	07/1963-09/1963	$5,172
1806	Cosmo Investors, Inc.		Carousel Restaurant	11/1963-01/1964	$10,990
1818	Owens Corning Fiberglass Corporation	Themselves	Building #11	02/1964-04/1964	$9,849
1840 (A-F)	Owens Corning Fiberglass Corporation	Themselves	Buildings #7 and #41	04/1964-08/1964	$19,035
1850	Park Union Corporation	Frank, Lindberg and Maki	Eastland Shopping Center	07/1964-12/1964	$204,844
1850 PNB	Park National Bank	Joseph Baker and Associates	Park National Bank	07/1964-11/1964	$9,430
1860	Southgate Development Corporation	Frank, Lindberg and Maki	Southgate Corners Shopping Center	06/1964-12/1964	$187,001
1863 A, B	Owens Corning Fiberglass Corporation	Owens Corning	Building #27	07/1964-10/1964	$45,586
1864	Jeffers Brothers		Store Fronts	07/1964-08/1964	$7,669
1870	McDonnell's Shoe Store	Orville Varasso	McDonnell's Shoe Store	09/1964-12/1964	$12,251

JOB NUMBER	NAME, OWNER, AGENT AND/OR BUSINESS	ARCHITECT	BUILDING	MONTH/ YEAR(S) BUILT	COST
1881	Coca-Cola	Joseph Baker and Associates	Coca-Cola Plant	02/1965-07/1965	$111.759
1898	Sherwin Williams Company, James O. Austin	Orville Varasso	Sherwin Williams Paint Store	06/1965-08/1965	$30,519
1900	Seaway Store, G and R Realty Company	Frank, Lindberg and Maki	Seaway, Newark	03/1965-10/1965	$125,788
1901	Ragal Corporation, Merchandising	Orville Varasso	Merchandising	05/1965-11/1965	$73,019
1911	Baker, Joseph	Joseph Baker and Associates	Joseph Baker Office	09/1965-01/1966	$23,645
1919	Owens Corning Fiberglass Corporation.	Themselves	Building #26	10/1965-11/1965	$8,528
1925	Westhall Company		Hub Store	10/1965-011/1965	$8,498
1928	Newark Processing Company, Inc.		Newark Processing Building	11/1965-11/1965	$5,050
1930	Columbia Gas of Ohio, Inc.	Themselves	Columbia Gas Building	12/1965-05/1966	$71,650
1938	Newark Board of Education		Cherry Valley Elementary School	11/1965-12/1965	$5,250
1945	Holy Trinity Lutheran Church	Frederick Stritzel	Holy Trinity Lutheran Church	04/1965-11/1966	$103,602
1950	Egan Funeral Home	Orville Varasso	Egan Funeral Home	04/1966-09/1966	$77,450
1955	Kentucky Fried Chicken	Mrs. W. A. Jacobs	Kentucky Fried Chicken	05/1966-08/1966	$31,972
1960	Grady, Jim	Jack E. Titus	Jim Grady Pontiac, Inc.	07/1966-11/1966	$33,518
1963	Licking Laundry Company Inc.	Orville Varasso	Licking Laundry Plant	07/1966-09/1966	$8,730
1965	Walker, Raymond and Battat, Robert, BF . Goodrich	A. A. Stavoli	B. F. Goodrich Store	08/1966-01/1967	$115,000
1970	WCLT, Inc.	Schooley, Cornelius and Schooley	WCLT Radio Station	08/1966-12/1966	$29,343

JOB NUMBER	NAME, OWNER, AGENT AND/OR BUSINESS	ARCHITECT	BUILDING	MONTH/ YEAR(S) BUILT	COST
1971	B and L Motor Freight, Inc.	Orville Varasso and Associates	Office	10/1966-04/1967	$33,772
1990	Sears Building, Thirty Three West Main Corporation	Orville Varasso and Associates	Sears Building	02/1967-08/1967	$85,075
1991	Seaway Store, G and R Realty Company	Frank, Lindberg and Maki	Sea Way, Washington Court House	03/1967-08/1967	$175,679
1993	Neal Avenue Methodist Church		Neal Avenue Methodist Church	03/1967-04/1967	$5,932
2000	Federal Mogul Corporation, Newark Ohio Industrial Park, Inc.	Frank, Lindberg and Maki	Federal Mogul	07/1967-12/1967	$131,047
2000-X	Federal Mogul Corporation, Newark Ohio Industrial Park, Inc.	Frank, Lindberg and Maki	Federal Mogul	12/1967-03/1968	$4,413
2002	King's Department Store, Hull, Eli Estate c/o George McDonald		King's Department Store	05/1967-07/1967	$7,617
2010	Adjutant General's Department, U.S.P. and F.O., State of Ohio	Joseph Baker and Associates	National Guard Warehouse	09/1967-07/1968	$267,796
2012	Public Finance Company, Arcade Realty	Public Finance Sketch	Public Finance	07/1967-08/1967	$11,809
2020	YWCA of Licking County	Joseph Baker and Associates	YWCA	09/1967-03/1969	$716,885
2021	Federal Mogul Corporation, Newark Ohio Industrial Park, Inc.	Chicago Bridge and Iron Company	Federal Mogul	12/1967-02/1968	$8,960
2022	Kaydan, Inc., Industrial Automotive		Industrial Automotive	02/1968-03/1968	$7,563
2030	Walker, Raymond and Battat, Robert, BF. Goodrich	A. A. Stavoli	B. F. Goodrich Store	07/1968-09/1968	$18,100
2034	Vercoe and Company		Vercoe and Company Office	05/1968-05/1968	$5,947

JOB NUMBER	NAME, OWNER, AGENT AND/OR BUSINESS	ARCHITECT	BUILDING	MONTH/ YEAR(S) BUILT	COST
2035	Soldiers and Sailors Memorial Building, Auditorium		Auditorium Building	05/1968-06/1968	$4,482
2036	G and R Realty Company		Minit-Man Car Wash	06/1968-08/1968	$5,540
2039	Park National Bank	Joseph Baker and Associates	Park National Bank	10/1968-12/1968	$6,364
2040	Dow Chemical Corporation, Newark Ohio Industrial Park, Inc.	Frank, Lindberg and Maki	Dow Chemical Building	08/1968-11/1969	$493,059
2044	Dow Chemical Corporation, Newark Ohio Industrial Park, Inc.	Dow Chemical Corporation	Dow Chemical Building	10/1968-12/1968	$15,113
2048	Dow Chemical Corporation, Newark Ohio Industrial Park, Inc.	Dow Chemical Corporation	Process Structure	09/1969-09/1969	$272,367
2050	Fairfield Scientific Corporation, Astro Fireworks Plant	Joseph Baker and Associates	Packing Building	12/1968-06/1969	$49,927
2052	Dow Chemical Corporation, Newark Ohio Industrial Park, Inc.	The Dow Chemical Corporation	Saranex Enclosure	05/1969-07/1969	$36,379
2053	Yost, William T. Company	Orville Varasso and Associates	Office and Warehouse	05/1969-09/1969	$62,184
2055	National Hard Chrome Plating, Newark Ohio Industrial Park, Inc.	Jack Maki	National Hard Chrome Plating	07/1969-02/1970	$91,011
2060	Fairfield Scientific Corporation, Astro Fireworks Plant	Joseph Baker and Associates	Office Building and Machine Shop	08/1969-02/1970	$79,349
2062	American Legion Post #85	Orville Varasso and Associates	Cussins and Fearn Building	10/1969-02/1970	$34,363
2063	Newark Meat Supply, Inc.	Orville Varasso	Newark Meat Supply	11/1969-03/1970	$23,255

JOB NUMBER	NAME, OWNER, AGENT AND/OR BUSINESS	ARCHITECT	BUILDING	MONTH/ YEAR(S) BUILT	COST
2070	Adjutant General's Department, U.S.P. and F.O.,State of Ohio	Joseph Baker and Associates	Combined Support and Maintenance Shop	05/1970 *	*
2071	Dow Chemical Corporation, Newark Ohio Industrial Park, Inc.	Dow Chemical Corporation	Switchgear Building	03/1970-05/1970	$11,050
2080	Standard Register, Newark Ohio Industrial Park, Inc.	Jack Maki	Standard Register	06/1970 *	*

* Information not available

Appendix III

Jobs Not on the Job List

While searching the Advocate archives for articles and advertisements the jobs noted below were found. No job numbers were assigned to these.

The Year is Listed
Gibbs Garage 1947
Heisey Company Factory Addition 1947
Hulls Newark Wallpaper Store 1947
Moore's Stores 1957
New Bleachers South Side of White Field 1947
New Sidewalks around the Newark City Building 1951
Pitts Lincoln Mercury 1950s
Scott Furniture Store remodel 1947

The Year is Not Listed
Christian Science Church
Heath Village Fire Station
Mt. Union Township School Addition Coshocton County
Park Hotel, Coshocton, Restoration Following a Fire
Purity School, Licking County

Appendix IV

Buckey Brothers Bids 1947 - 1966

The winning bidder for a job is in capital letters so BUCKEY BROTHERS INC, shows they got the job. The bidding process has its own set of rules. The lowest bidder is not always the one that gets the job. The highest and lowest bids are sometimes discarded and other factors affect who gets the work.

DATE	JOB	WORK	ARCHITECT		BIDDERS	BID
9-1947	120	Laundry Building, State Hospital		1.	BUCKEY BROTHERS, INC.	$133,962.00
		Mt. Vernon, Ohio		2.	Knowlton Construction	$140,000.00
8-1948	240	Elementary School		1.	BUCKEY BROTHERS, INC.	$119,818.00
		Utica, Ohio		2.	Norton and Nadalin	$129,800.00
				3.	W. J. Camlin Company	$143,960.00
				4.	Kent Brothers	$147,270.00
				5.	James I. Barnes	$167,900.00
8-1948	*	Alterations to Employee Dining Room.		1.	BUCKEY BROTHERS, INC.	$18,412.00
		Mt. Vernon State Hospital				
		Mt. Vernon , Ohio				
9-1948	*	Industrial Arts Building.		1.	BUCKEY BROTHERS, INC.	$39,976.00
		Hebron, Ohio		2.	W. J. Camlin Company.	$43,562.00
				3.	A. L. Meyers Construction	$44,937.00
5-1949	*	Additions to Union School		1.	BUCKEY BROTHERS, INC.	$50,784.00
		Nellie, Ohio		2.	M. Jacobs	$51,846.00
6-1949	335	Addition to Newark Township School		1.	BUCKEY BROTHERS, INC.	$21,475.00
		Newark, Ohio		2.	W. J. Camlin Company	$29,419.00
5-1949	340	St. Francis de Sales Gymnasium		1.	W. J. Paul	$124,000.00
		Newark, Ohio		2.	BUCKEY BROTHERS, INC.	$137,000.00
				3.	W. J. Camlin Company	$149,000.00

6-1950	410	Alterations to Fulton School		1.	BUCKEY BROTHERS, INC.	$14,298.00
		Newark, Ohio		2.	W. J. Camlin Company	$14,842.00
8-1950	440	Auditorium and Gymnasium		1.	D. A. Gardner Construction	$92,744.00
		Newark Township (Fulton School)		2.	BUCKEY BROTHERS, INC.	$92,908.00
		Newark, Ohio		3.	W. J. Camlin Company	$99,993.00
				4.	O. J. Paul	$108,254.00
8-1950	433	Granville Shop Addition High School		1.	BUCKEY BROTHERS, INC.	$36,900.00
				2.	Westlake and Associates	$39,057.00
				3.	W. J. Camlin Company	$40,481.00
				4.	Knowlton Construction Company	$44,260.00
				5.	Joseph Skilken Company	$49,585.00
				6.	Norton and Nadalin	$53,780.00
		COMBINED BID		1.	Knowlton Construction Company	$318,600.00
		Granville Elementary and Granville Shop Addition		2.	BUCKEY BROTHERS, INC.	$319,300.00
				3.	W. J. Camlin Company	$339,823.00
				4.	Norton and Nadalin	$387,000.00
				5.	Joseph Skilken Company	$471,000.00
7-1950	435	Lincoln School Addition		1.	BUCKEY BROTHERS, INC.	$70,958.00
		Coshocton, Ohio		2.	C. W. Taylor and Son	$82,230.00
				3.	Edward T. Jacobs Construction	$86,729.00
				4.	W. H. Howard	$92,461.00
	436	Sycamore School Addition		1.	BUCKEY BROTHERS, INC.	$41,273.00
		Coshocton, Ohio		2.	C. W. Taylor & Son	$48,240.00
				3.	Salrin Construction	$52,009.00
				4.	W. H. Howard	$52,145.00
				5.	Edward T. Jacobs Construction	$52,300.00
		Washington School Addition		1.	Edward T. Jacobs Construction	$80,000.00
		Coshocton, Ohio		2.	W. H. Howard	$87,429.00
				3.	BUCKEY BROTHERS, INC.	$90,496.00

		COMBINED BID		1.	BUCKEY BROTHERS, INC.	$199,377.00
		Lincoln, Sycamore & Washington		2.	Edward T. Jacobs Construction	$218,000.00
		School Additions		3.	W. H. Howard	$229,035.00
6-1951	520	Addition to McKean Township Elementary		1.	Walter Chaney Construction	$36,995.00
		Licking County, Ohio		2.	BUCKEY BROTHERS, INC.	$37,476.00
6-1953	840	North Elementary School		1.	BUCKEY BROTHERS, INC.	$84,321.00
		Newark, Ohio		2.	Walter Chaney Construction	$87,951.00
				3.	W. J. Camlin Co.	$102,418.00
8-1953	860	Addition to Fulton School		1.	BUCKEY BROTHERS, INC.	$43,590.00
		Licking County		2.	W. J. Camlin Co.	$46,361.00
				3.	Edward T. Jacobs Construction	$51,893.00
2-1954	940	Benjamin Franklin Junior High School	Joseph Baker and Associates	1.	Walter Chaney Construction	$297,968.00
		Newark, Ohio		2.	BUCKEY BROTHERS, INC.	$299,589.00
				3.	Kent Brothers	$311,284.00
				4.	D. E. Gardner	$313,537.00
				5.	O. J. Paul	$321,245.00
				6.	W. J. Camlin Company	$327,389.00
8-1954	999	Granville Elementary		1.	BUCKEY BROTHERS, INC.	$134,864.00
		School Addition		2.	Knowlton Construction Company	$146,300.00
		Granville, Ohio		3.	Walter Chaney Construction	$148,927.00
				4.	Henry A. Justus	$150,744.00
				5.	Dawson - Evans Construction	$161,542.00
				6.	W. J. Camlin Company	$182,073.00

7-1955	1080	Madison Township School	Merle T. Orr and Associates	1.	Leroy Stuller	$72,000.00
		Newark, Ohio		2.	BUCKEY BROTHERS, INC.	$94,616.00
				3.	Walter Chaney Construction	$98,846.00
				4.	W. J. Camlin Company	$98,890.00
				5.	Harry E. Miller Construction	$107,583.00
				6.	Thomas Flannigan	$107,800.00
3-1956	1177	Saints Peter and Paul Seminary Building	Victor J. Basso	1.	BUCKEY BROTHERS, INC.	$208,900.00
		Hebron, Ohio		2.	Kraus and Pagura	$212,384.00
				3.	W. J. Camlin Company	$219,149.00
				4.	Altman - Coady Construction	$224,811.00
				5.	Walter Chaney Construction.	$228,468.00
				6.	Fred Kreutz and Sons	$228,719.00
				7.	L. E. Rusinger	$252,830.00
				8.	F and Y Building Service	$264,610.00
5-1956	1188	Bennington-Liberty School	Joseph Baker and Associates	1.	BUCKEY BROTHERS, INC.	$58,644.00
		Johnstown, Ohio		2.	C. W. Taylor and Sons	$60,960.00
				3.	Walter Chaney Construction.	$61,836.00
				4.	Oshel Robbins	$63,147.00
7-1956	1205	Heath School Bus Garage	Joseph Baker and Associates	1.	BUCKEY BROTHERS, INC.	$27,835.00
				2.	Walter Chaney Construction	$35,392.00
11-1956	1220	Perry School Addition	Joseph Baker and Associates	1.	BUCKEY BROTHERS, INC.	$31,513.00
		Licking County, Ohio		2.	Oshel Rollins	$35,224.00
				3	O. J. Paul	$35,816.00
				4.	Walter Chaney Construction	$36,248.00
				5.	C. W. Taylor and Sons	$39,980.00
1-1957	1230	Park National Bank	Joseph Baker and Associates	1.	BUCKEY BROTHERS, INC.	$578,116.00
		50 N. Third Street		2.	W. J. Camlin Company	$579,996.00
		Newark, Ohio		3.	Trapp Construction	$636,850.00
				4.	Gilmore - Olson	$690,000.00

9-1957	1275	Holy Trinity Lutheran Church	Frederick Stritzel	1.	BUCKEY BROTHERS, INC.	$84,413.00
		(Education Unit), Newark, Ohio		2.	H. H. Simpson and Son	$85,790.00
				3.	W. J. Camlin Company	$87,900.00
				4.	Walter Chaney Construction	$98,208.00
9-1958	1313	Lakewood High School	Joseph Baker and Associates	1.	BUCKEY BROTHERS, INC.	$389,716.00
		Hebron, Ohio		2.	C. W. Taylor and Sons	$394,440.00
				3.	O. J. Paul	$398,500.00
				4.	E. V. Taylor	$399,285.00
				5.	Walter Chaney Construction	$399,946.00
				6.	Kent Brothers	$409,100.00
				7.	Jen and Churella	$409,629.00
				8.	Sever-Williams	$418,000.00
				9.	Harry E. Miller	$427,560.00
				10.	Miller Construction	$429,781.00
				11.	Krause and Pagura	$430,128.00
				12.	Fred Kreutz	$437,000.00
				13.	W. J. Camlin Company	$440,882.00
				14.	Ang Construction	$486,600.00
				15.	E. Mast and Son	$488,969.00
12-1966	2020	YWCA of Licking County	Joseph Baker and Associates	1.	Walter Chaney Construction	$549,386.00
		Newark, Ohio		2.	Paul Construction	$554,800.00
				3.	BUCKEY BROTHERS, INC.	$566,000.00
				4.	W. J. Camlin Company	$574,400.00
				5.	R. A. Bergs	$589,841.00
				6.	John J. O'Neill Company	$590,000.00
12-1966	1960	Jim Grady Pontiac, Inc.	J. E. Titus	1.	Dominion Development	$34,591.16
		Newark, Ohio		2.	BUCKEY BROTHERS, INC.	$36,660.00
				3.	Don Oxley and Associates	$41,633.00
				4.	Walter Chaney Construction	$42,400.00
				5.	Ora E. Warner	$43,469.00
				6.	John J. O'Neill Company	$43,736.00

Photo Index

DEDICATION

CHAPTER I

CHAPTER 2

Photo Index continues on next page...

ACKNOWLEDGMENTS

After looking at my father's collection of files and papers stored in boxes, it was time to organize them into something useful. A website was started but never finished. Thanks to this start many photos and newspaper articles had already been scanned into the computer, but where does one begin writing a book?

Ron Sherwood and I started by finding the addresses for the buildings on the Jobs in Alphabetical Order list. This was done at the Granville Historical Society's office where we could access their city directories and older telephone books to secure most of the addresses. If available the address is given at a place and time when the construction was completed. Later as the area changed some addresses are given as Heath addresses. Then in casual conversations with friends some addresses were located, others were obtained by driving to the locations.

Next came the computer work. Typing the jobs as listed in the appendices was a problem. I was directed by John Kennedy, from the "Licking County Computer Society" now known as the East-Central Ohio Technology Users Club, to Lori Brown who teaches a computer class for the club. Thank you Lori for help in setting up tables. Now I was on my way.

A visit to the Downtown Newark Licking County Library to find more Buckey information was the next step. Thank you Cory Stutes for getting me started with the Newark Advocate archives. Lindsay Kelley was most helpful, not only helping with computer problems, but directing me in the right direction when I had problems searching the archives. Tony Miceli was instrumental in the early stages of the book with computer help and informing me that I needed documentation for the photos, articles and advertisements.

Thank you Robert McGaughy for your help particularly with photo identification. You took the time to show photos, with no identification, to your friends and to various meetings where you were quite successful finding names for unidentified people in some of the older photos. Your search for a photo of the Lustron house you once lived in was appreciated.

Meeting at the office of Southgate Corporation with Robert O'Neill I was pleased to obtain the current addresses for the Buckey built buildings in the Hebron Industrial Park, formerly Newark Ohio Industrial Park. Thank you for these contributions to the book.

Sara Heiser, a neighbor, helped with the book by typing the jobs R. E, Buckey bid on from 1947 to 1966. No record from the bids from 1966 to 1970 were found among the Buckey papers.

Karen Richards and Eric Richards, grandchildren of R. E. Buckey, supported the writing by proof reading the book as it progressed. I am most grateful to Elaine Long for editing the book.

And the last-minute rush to find photos. Thank you Emily Larson for sharing photos from the Licking County Historical Society. Your search for a couple of needed photos was appreciated, and they were found. Briana Stone, from the Park National Bank, was able to meet a deadline for photos. Roberta Buckey Richards went through her Buckey papers and at the last minute contributed the final photos.

Special thanks go to Aaron Keirns of Little River Publishing. I chose him because of the way he coordinates the text with the photos and his fine attention to detail.

Have a Question or Comment?

Please use the Facebook Page where you may post a photo of a Buckey-built building. No photos were available for many buildings when the book was written and you could contribute here. Perhaps your relative worked for the brothers and you could tell about his or her experience.

Facebook Site
Buckey Brothers Building a Community

Email Address
If you have a question or a statement about the Buckey Brothers, use this email address: Buckeybrothers@hotmail.com

COVER PHOTOS DOCUMENTATION

Front cover building photos:

Top left: The Park National Bank (Job 1230).

Top right: Saints Peter and Paul Seminary (Job 1177).

Bottom: Seaway Store, Newark (Job 1900).

Back cover building photos:

Top left: B&L Motor Freight (Job 1971).

Top right: Lakewood High School (Job 1313).

Middle left: Benjamin Franklin Junior High School (Job 940).

Middle right: Newark Township Fire Station #2 (Job 610).

Bottom left: Huffman Motor Sales (Job 3).

Bottom right: Sears Building (Job 1990).

All cover photos from the Buckey family collection.

Made in the USA
Columbia, SC
26 August 2019